We the people of the United States, in order to form a more perfect Union, establish justice, insure domestic tranquility, provide for the common defense, promote the general welfare, and secure the blessings of liberty to ourselves and our posterity, do ordain and establish this Constitution for the United States of America.

(Preamble to the U.S. Constitution)

We hold these truths to be self-evident, that all men are created equal, that they are endowed by their Creator with certain inalienable Rights, that among these are Life, Liberty and the pursuit of Happiness.

(From the Declaration of Independence)

Congress shall make no law respecting an establishment of religion, or prohibiting the free exercise thereof; or abridging the freedom of speech, or of the press; or the right of the people peaceably to assemble, and to petition the Government for a redress of grievances.

(Article One, the Bill of Rights, the Constitution of the United States of America)

Blessed is the nation whose God is the Lord.

(Ps. 33:12)

PRAYERS THAT PREVAIL FOR AMERICA

Changing a Nation Through Prayer

PRAYERS THAT PREVAIL FOR AMERICA

Changing a Nation Through Prayer

By
Clift Richards & Lloyd Hildebrand

Victory House, Inc.
Tulsa, Oklahoma

Unless otherwise indicated, all Scripture quotations are taken from the *King James Version* of the Bible.

Scripture quotations marked NIV are taken from the *New International Version*. Those passages are taken from the HOLY BIBLE: NEW INTERNATIONAL VERSION © 1978 by the New York International Bible Society, used by permission of Zondervan Bible Publishers.

Prayers are paraphrased from these versions unless otherwise stated.

PRAYERS THAT PREVAIL FOR AMERICA
Changing a Nation Through Prayer
Copyright © 1993 by K & C International, Inc.
ISBN 0-932081-34-7
All rights reserved
Printed in the United States of America

Published by Victory House, Inc.
P. O. Box 700238
Tulsa, Oklahoma 74170
(918) 747-5009

CONTENTS

ONE NATION UNDER GOD

The highest glory of the American Revolution was this: It connected, in one indissoluble bond, the principles of civil government with the principles of Christianity. (John Quincy Adams)

The light of God's love brightened the western skies after the New World was discovered. The hearts of many oppressed Europeans filled with hope as they looked beyond the western horizon and caught a vision of a new land where liberty would be the highest value.

They watched. They waited. They prayed and they planned. As always, God heard their cries and He began to prepare a marvelous miracle for His people. The situation was similar in some respects to the time when the Hebrews were held as slaves by the Egyptians.

And the Lord said, I have surely seen the affliction of my people..., and have heard their cry by reason of their task masters; for I know their sorrows; And I am come down to deliver them..., and to bring them up out of that land...unto a land flowing with milk and honey. (Exod. 3:7-8)

God heard the cries of the Israelites. They prayed and He responded. The intercession of their leader, Moses, moved God's heart. He delivered them from slavery and brought them into the Promised Land.

1

The United States of America is an answer to the prayers of people who wanted to be able to worship Him freely. Walt Whitman said, "The United States is the world's greatest poem." It is also the world's greatest miracle. It is the modern-day version of "a land flowing with milk and honey."

People wanted to be able to worship God according to their consciences. At the same time, God was looking for a people who would put Him first in their hearts and in their national affairs — one nation under God.

Great expectancy filled the air over the European continent as God's voice resonated above the waves of the Atlantic Ocean, calling believers to a new land and a new day. Thousands heard His voice and they responded with bravery and obedience. These valiant pilgrims ventured forth, following in the footsteps of Father Abraham who heard a similar call long before:

> *Now the Lord had said unto Abram, Get thee out of thy country, and from thy kindred, and from thy father's house, unto a land that I will shew thee: And I will make of thee a great nation, and I will bless thee, and make thy name great; and thou shalt be a blessing. (Gen. 12:1-2)*

The New World beckoned and God had a special purpose for America. Freedom would be the password and worship was the key that would open "the golden door" to so many who had been oppressed for so long. The words of Emma Lazarus's famous poem, inscribed at the base of the Statue of Liberty, beautifully portray God's call:

> Give me your tired, your poor, your huddled masses yearning to breathe free, the

wretched refuse of your teeming shore. Send these, the homeless, tempest-tost to me, I lift my lamp beside the golden door! (Emma Lazarus, 1883)

They came to the land of promise in droves — from England, France, Italy, Germany, Ireland, Holland, Spain and elsewhere. God kept calling and they heard His voice. He continued to respond to believing prayer. The Baptists, under Roger Williams, founded Rhode Island. The Society of Friends (Quakers), led by William Penn, colonized Pennsylvania. Roman Catholics found a safe haven in Maryland. Puritan dissenters from Great Britain enjoyed their new-found freedom in New England. Methodists, Presbyterians, Mennonites, Lutherans, Anglicans and members of other sects, including those of Jewish background, came. Though there was great diversity in some of their beliefs, they shared a common goal: they were seeking the Promised Land where they could worship God in spirit and in truth.

But the hour cometh, and now is, when the true worshippers shall worship the Father in spirit and in truth: for the Father seeketh such to worship him. God is a Spirit: and they that worship him must worship him in spirit and in truth. (John 4:23-24)

The Puritan people firmly believed that America was their Promised Land. They took a verse from the Sermon on the Mount to describe their new homeland: "Ye are the light of the world. A city that is set on an hill cannot be hid" (Matt. 5:14). America — a city set on an hill, the Promised Land, a land flowing with milk and honey, the world's greatest miracle and an answered prayer. The "sweet land of liberty" was destined to have a special purpose in God's plans for the world.

The Cornerstone of Society

At his first presidential inauguration, General George Washington inserted the words "So help me God" into the Oath of Office for the Presidency of the United States. As our nation's first president, he later wrote, "It is impossible to govern...without God and the Bible." All the presidents after him — Episcopalians, Presbyterians, Unitarians, Dutch Reformed, Methodists, Disciples of Christ, Baptists, Congregationalists, Quakers and a Roman Catholic — have recognized this same fundamental truth and all have followed Washington's example by stating, "So help me God," thereby recognizing that their high office is a sacred trust.

Yes, as Washington pointed out, the Bible is the foundation cornerstone of our society. From the Word of God we have formed our value system regarding family living, worship, hard work, personal responsibility, justice, compassion and wisdom. For more than two centuries the principles of the Bible have guided our nation — through a Civil War, a Great Depression, two World Wars, the Cold War and the nuclear age.

Each of our presidents has affirmed his personal belief in Almighty God and the power of prayer. When D-day had to be postponed due to inclement weather conditions, General Dwight Eisenhower found an antidote for his anxiety through prayer. Later, he wrote:

> If there was nothing else in my life to prove
> the existence of an almighty and merciful God,
> the events of the next twenty-four hours did it.

This is what I found out about religion: It gives you the courage to make the decisions you must make in a crisis, and then the confidence to leave the results to higher power. Only by trust in oneself and trust in God can a man carrying responsibility find repose.

Judeo-Christian Values

In an effort to show respect for the "pluralism" of our society, many people today are losing sight of the Bible-based principles on which our nation was founded. They have forgotten the words of the Psalmist, "Blessed is the nation whose God is the Lord" (Ps. 33:12), and in the process of secularization, our nation is drifting perilously close to the description of a godless, idolatrous society portrayed by the Apostle Paul:

> *Because that, when they knew God, they glorified him not as God, neither were thankful; but became vain in their imaginations, and their foolish heart was darkened. Professing themselves to be wise, they became fools, And changed the glory of the uncorruptible God into an image made like to corruptible man, and to birds, and fourfooted beasts, and creeping things. Wherefore God also gave them up to uncleanness through the lusts of their own hearts, to dishonour their own bodies between themselves: Who changed the truth of God into a lie, and worshipped and served the creature more than the Creator. (Rom. 1:21-25)*

Those who worship the creature more than the Creator are known as humanists, and it is humanistic secularization that threatens to undo our society in this modern age. During the twentieth century we have seen the Bible and prayers removed from our public schools, we have witnessed the intrusion of government into the affairs of religion and the Church, and we have watched Paul's catalog of sins (as depicted in Romans 1) displayed in open mockery of the Judeo-Christian ethic. The list of flagrant sins and abuses is endless: homosexuality, abortion, crime, violence, rape, fornication, wickedness, lawlessness, disobedience, infidelity, etc. Many are being deceived by a philosophy that is as godless as communism.

In a *Newsweek* article entitled, "Losing Our Moral Umbrella," Kenneth L. Woodward points out, "A nation at war [World War II] needed religious harmony. During the subsequent cold war against communism, the idea of a shared Judeo-Christian tradition was central to the era's politics of cohesion. 'Our government has no sense unless it is founded on a deeply religious faith,' President Dwight D. Eisenhower remarked....In his classic 1955 study, 'Protestant-Catholic-Jew,' the philosopher Will Herberg, a former communist, celebrated an adhesive American faith based on the triunion of the nation's major traditions. Although Jews were numerically much the shortest leg on this ecumenical stool, most non-Orthodox leaders welcomed the opportunities that interreligious dialogue and cooperation provided. Anti-Semitism was, by common conviction, outlawed as anti-American. Differences in doctrine mattered less than the fact that Jews and Christians shared the same Bible, insisted on monotheism and taught that both the individual and society stood under the judgment of the same God. Jesus, after all, was himself a Jew."

Woodward went on to show how this thinking is undergoing a radical change in the present time. Instead of the Judeo-Christian ethic which is woven into the very fiber of our nation, the doctrine of secular pluralism suggests that there are no longer any religious commonalities among the American people. Woodward observes, "But the real irony is that the idea of a common Judeo-Christian tradition is, for the United States at least, already outmoded." (See *Newsweek*, December 7, 1992, page 60.)

Church, we need to pray for our nation! The qualities that have enabled the United States to endure are being undermined from within. It is time for us to heed the warning of Paul:

> *Awake thou that sleepest, and arise from the dead, and Christ shall give thee light. See then that ye walk circumspectly, not as fools, but as wise, Redeeming the time, because the days are evil. Wherefore be ye not unwise, but understanding what the will of the Lord is. (Eph. 5:14-17)*

The Wall of Separation

There is a myth that influences many of our leaders and citizens in the present age. It involves the doctrine of the separation of church and state. The concept stems from the first article in the Bill of Rights of the U.S. Constitution:

> *Congress shall make no law respecting an establishment of religion, or prohibiting the free exercise thereof; or abridging the freedom of speech, or of the press; or the right of the people*

*peaceably to assemble, and to petition the
Government for a redress of grievances.*

This amendment to our constitution clearly states that
our legislators may not pass laws concerning the
establishment of any religion or prohibit anyone from
freely practicing their religious beliefs. *It does not put forth
the following ideas:*

1. Christians should not become involved in
   government.
2. There should always be an impenetrable
   wall between church and state.
3. The church should not endeavor to influence
   the government.
4. Christians should not pray for their
   government.
5. There should be no Bibles or prayers in
   government buildings and public schools.

To the contrary, this amendment actually encourages
citizens to freely enjoy their rights to worship, to speak
freely, to use the press, to peaceably assemble and to
petition the government. As Christians, we should become
actively involved in politics and in prayer so that our nation
can regain the protection of its moral umbrella.

The U.S. Constitution does not use the phrase "wall
of separation." This was coined by Thomas Jefferson in
1802. It is important to realize that Jefferson did not mean
that God was to be separated from government but rather
that government should not have control over the church
or religious practices.

Our forefathers were very sensitive to this issue
because many of them had come from countries where

there was a state church that often looked down upon religious minorities, persecuting them or even banning them altogether. In many European nations government and the church were inextricably entwined and many times this relationship led to political intrigue, immorality and injustice.

In the United States there can be no "state church," and it is against the law for the government to prohibit the free exercise of religion. However, it is very important for us in this modern age to realize that our founding fathers viewed the free exercise of religion through the clear lens of Judeo-Christian values. They were not envisioning the free exercise of dark religions and cults such as satanism and other occultic orientations.

The founding fathers actually promulgated Judeo-Christian values in their speeches and writings; even the earliest documents of our nation's government reflected these values with direct statements advocating faith in God and adherence to the Scriptures. They expected schools and institutions of America to freely embrace and encourage Judeo-Christian values.

Certainly it is not against the law for the Church to influence government (through prayer, freedom of speech, freedom of the press, the right to assemble, and the right to petition our government). In all these ways, Christians need to become very active today.

One crucial way in which we can bring to bear a godly influence in our land is to campaign for the election of committed Christian people to various government offices.

The first Chief Justice of the United States Supreme Court, John Jay, wrote, "Providence has given to our people the choice of their rulers, and it is the duty...of a Christian nation to select and prefer Christians for their rulers.'' Justice Jay, an interpreter of the laws of our land, said this is *our duty*.

The Word of God sounds a clear warning to Americans today:

> *At what instant I shall speak concerning a nation, and concerning a kingdom, to pluck up, and to pull down, and to destroy it; If that nation, against whom I have pronounced, turn from their evil, I will repent of the evil that I thought to do unto them. And at what instant I shall speak concerning a nation, and concerning a kingdom, to build and to plant it; If it do evil in my sight, that it obey not my voice, then I will repent of the good, wherewith I said I would benefit them. (Jer. 18:7-10)*

God's blessing is promised to our nation if we will:

1. Turn from our evil.

2. Obey the voice of God.

These two prerequisites need to be the focus of our intercessions in behalf of America today. The topical prayers in *Prayers That Prevail for America* keep these goals in mind. God will hear and answer our prayers and the result will be that He will continue to build and plant our nation so that we will be able to enjoy all His benefits and be a blessing to the world.

If America fails in this divine challenge, if the Church of Jesus Christ fails America in this hour, then we will be judged. God's judgment comes to a nation in a variety of ways: through warfare, natural disasters, famine, economic collapse and plagues. Has that judgment already begun?

Daniel Webster wrote, "Whatever makes a man a good Christian also makes him a good citizen." Good Christians are good stewards of all God gives to them, and the privilege of citizenship in the United States of America is one of the greatest gifts of all. Therefore, we do need to get involved through intercessory prayer and persistent, relentless and loving action in this crucial hour.

What Does the Bible Say?

The following Scriptures show how God deals with nations, and the godly principles that make a nation great:

> *The word of the Lord came to me: "Son of man, if a country sins against me by being unfaithful and I stretch out my hand against it to cut off its food supply and send famine upon it and kill its men and their animals, even if these three men — Noah, Daniel and Job — were in it, they could save only themselves by their righteousness, declares the Sovereign Lord. (Ezek. 14:12-14, NIV)*

> *See, I have taught you decrees and laws as the Lord my God commanded me, so that you may follow them in the land you are entering to take possession of it. Observe them carefully, for this will show your wisdom and understanding to the nations, who will hear about all these decrees and say, "Surely this great nation is a wise and understanding people." What other nation is so great as to have*

their gods near them the way the Lord our God is near us whenever we pray to him? And what other nation is so great as to have such righteous decrees and laws as this body of laws I am setting before you today? (Deut. 4:5-8, NIV)

Remember me, O Lord, when you show favor to your people, come to my aid when you save them, that I may enjoy the prosperity of your chosen ones, that I may share in the joy of your nation and join your inheritance in giving praise. (Ps. 106:4-5, NIV)

It is a land the Lord your God cares for; the eyes of the Lord your God are continually on it from the beginning of the year to its end. So if you faithfully obey the commands I am giving you today — to love the Lord your God and to serve him with all your heart and with all your soul — then I will send rain on your land in its season, both autumn and spring rains, so that you may gather in your grain, new wine and oil. I will provide grass in the fields for your cattle, and you will eat and be satisfied. (Deut. 11:12-17, NIV)

God's Word is clear. A nation will be blessed when God is the center of its national life. Nations that turn away from God will be judged.

Let's join together and ask God to lead the United States of America to always be the land He cares for. May His eyes continually be upon our land, from the beginning of each year to the end of each year. (See Deut. 11:12.)

Let's pray for our people, asking God to lead all of us to hearken diligently unto His commandments so that our nation will become a God-fearing, God-honoring land once more.

The Church's Response

In what ways can the Church become a part of God's answer to the prayers for our nation? The following suggestions are a partial list of answers that is based on the principles of the Word of God and the U.S. Constitution:

1.   Study the history of our nation.

2.   Stay informed concerning current events.

3.   Study the issues related to elections to find out what each candidate stands for and believes.

4.   Study your Bible daily.

5.   Be actively involved in the ministry of your local church.

6.   Live a godly and righteous life.

Then you will be properly equipped to effectively:

7.   Pray for our leaders.

8.   Pray for our people.

9.   Pray for revival in our land.

10.   Communicate with government officials — members of congress, the president, your governor, state legislators, local officials, etc. (Write letters, make phone calls, send telegrams or FAX's about issues on which you are informed and feel strongly.)

11.   Write letters to the editors of newspapers and periodicals. Call radio and TV talk shows to express the Christian point-of-view concerning the vital moral issues of our times.

12.   Attend public meetings of boards, commissions, councils, etc.

13.   Openly protest (through peaceable, lawful demonstrations and other God-honoring means) those practices in our society that oppose God's will.

14.   Vote in every election and encourage other godly citizens to register and vote. Support and vote for candidates who stand for godly principles.

15.   Run for public office — especially school boards and local public and party offices. Change and revival begin at the grass roots — at home.

16.   Teach your children and young people (as well as others, youth and adults) the principles of God's Word and the Christian heritage of our nation. (They won't get this in public school, and those who are ignorant of history are doomed to repeat it.)

17.   Volunteer to serve others.

18.   Fellowship with other Christians.

19.   Pay taxes, tithe, become debt-free, save money, and ask God to prosper you financially.

20.   Donate to ministries and support reputable Christian organizations working to effect change in public policy and to care for the victims of persecution, abuse, famine, natural disaster, sickness and poverty.

21. Become an agent of change in society, not just a complainer.

Jesus said, "Ye are the salt of the earth: but if the salt have lost his savour, wherewith shall it be salted? it is thenceforth good for nothing, but to be cast out, and to be trodden under foot of men. Ye are the light of the world. A city that is set on an hill cannot be hid. Neither do men light a candle, and put it under a bushel, but on a candlestick; and it giveth light unto all that are in the house. Let your light so shine before men, that they may see your good works, and glorify your Father which is in heaven" (Matt. 5:13-16).

Our Master also revealed to us, by His own life and His teaching, that the greatest witness we can give to our society is one of love:

> *A new commandment I give unto you, That ye love one another; as I have loved you, that ye also love one another. By this shall all men know that ye are my disciples, if ye have love one to another. (John 13:34-35)*

God loves the United States of America. His light has guided our nation through the years. As we enter into His plan for our country through prayer and action we need to remember to:

1. Let our light shine (by reflecting God's light) so that people will glorify our Father in heaven.

2. Love as Jesus has loved us so that all men will know that we are His disciples.

> *Spare thy people, O Lord, and give not*
> *thine heritage to reproach, that the heathen*
> *should rule over them.* *(Joel 2:17)*

Our God-Inspired Constitution

The Constitution of the United States is a document that was bathed in prayer by our founding fathers. For many days the framers of the constitution argued and debated about its organization and its wording. This led the entire New York delegation to leave the meetings altogether. Such disunity caused a pall of gloom to settle over the meetings.

Eighty-one-year-old Benjamin Franklin, so ill that he had to be carried into the meeting hall, stood to address the discouraged delegates. He reminded them of earlier meetings of the Provincial Congress which had always opened with prayer. In the first meeting of the Provincial Congress (in 1774), for example, the founding fathers met for more than three hours in earnest prayer for the nation and their deliberations before they began their planning. George Washington, John Adams, Patrick Henry and many other well-known leaders knelt before the Lord, seeking His blessings on America.

After reminding them of the power of prayer that they had experienced during the meetings of the Provincial Congress, Ben Franklin went on to call the delegates to the Constitutional Convention to intercession: "In the beginning of the contest with Great Britain, when we were sensible of danger, we had daily prayer in this room for divine protection. Our prayers, sir, were heard and they were graciously answered. . . . And have we now forgotten this powerful Friend? Or do we imagine that we no longer need His assistance?

"I've lived, sir, a long time, and the longer I live, the more convincing proofs I see of this truth: That God governs in the affairs of men. If a sparrow cannot fall to the ground without His notice, is it probable that an empire can rise without His aid? We've been assured in the sacred writings that unless the Lord build the house, they labor in vain who build it. I firmly believe this, and I also believe that without His concurring aid, we shall succeed in this political building no better than the builders of Babel.

"I therefore beg leave to move that henceforth prayers imploring the assistance of Heaven and its blessing on our deliberations be held in this assembly every morning before we proceed to business."

As a result of Franklin's affirmation of the power of prayer in the Constitutional Convention, several wonderful and amazing things happened. The entire assembly of delegates participated in three days of prayer and fasting. They joined together and visited every church they could find in Philadelphia in order to seek God's face and hear His Word proclaimed. When they reconvened, many delegates later reported, every unfriendly feeling had been expelled! Unity was restored. The decision-making flowed without friction. It was a dramatic turning point for the development of our nation — and the U.S. Constitution was born!

Also, as a result of Franklin's call to prayer, chaplains were established in the House of Representatives and the Senate to ensure that God's blessings would be invoked before all their meetings.

Incidentally, at the earlier Congress Franklin referred to (the Provincial Congress of 1774), the delegates actually prayed the Word of God (Psalms 35, in fact) before they proceeded with their business. One verse of this Psalm of David states: "I will give thee thanks in the great congregation: I will praise thee among much people" (Ps. 35:18).

In the early days of our nation, the presidents and the congress frequently called the people to prayer, fasting and thanksgiving. Many national days of prayer were observed, and businesses would close in recognition of the nation's need for prayer. The U.S. Congress even went so far as to keep a record of answered prayers in the Congressional Record. May it be that way once again.

Let us follow the faith-filled, God-fearing example of our founding fathers as we, like them, learn to pray the Word of God for our nation.

THE PRESIDENTS AND PRAYER

Almighty God, as we stand here at this moment, my future associates in the executive branch of our government join me in beseeching that Thou will make full and complete our dedication to the service of the people in this throng and their fellow citizens everywhere.

Give us, we pray, the power to discern clearly right from wrong, and allow all our words and actions to be governed thereby, and by the laws of this land. Especially we pray that our concern shall be for all the people regardless of station, race or calling. (Prayer given by President Dwight David Eisenhower prior to his inauguration.)

Nearly all the Presidents of the United States have found great power through prayer. The awesome responsibilities they face on a daily basis help them to realize that they need God's strength and wisdom to adequately administer the affairs of our nation. During the Civil War, for example, President Abraham Lincoln stated, "I am oftimes driven to my knees by the overwhelming conviction that I have nowhere else to go."

President Benjamin Harrison echoed the same truth when he wrote, "Prayer steadies one when he is walking in slippery places." This trust-in-prayer theme was reiterated by President Lyndon Baines Johnson, "No man could live in the house where I live and work without needing and seeking the support of earnest and frequent prayer....Prayer has helped me to bear the burdens of the first office, which are too great to be borne by anyone alone."

It was George Washington who added the words "So help me God" to the prescribed oath of office that is administered to each president-elect on Inauguration Day. This pledge has been accepted by all the presidents thereafter.

When his predecessor, President Franklin Delano Roosevelt, died, President Harry S. Truman, a Baptist, asked the representatives of the media to pray for him (if they ever prayed, which he said he doubted greatly!). Throughout his tenure as president, Truman often referred to his reliance on the power of prayer to sustain him.

Every President of the United States has affirmed his belief in God even though some of them were not formal members of a particular church or denomination. It has been said that "there are no atheists in foxholes," and it would appear that we could similarly state, "There are no atheists in the White House."

In view of these affirmations of faith on the part of our presidents and their trust in and practice of prayer, it is clear that our national motto, "In God We Trust," held profound meaning for each of them.

President William McKinley wrote, "The men who established this government had faith in God and sublimely trusted in Him. They besought His counsel and advice in every step of their progress. And so it has been ever since;

American history abounds in instances of this trait of piety, this sincere reliance on a Higher Power in all great trials in our national affairs. Our rulers may not always be observers of the outward forms of religion, but we have never had a president, from Washington to Harrison, who publicly avowed infidelity, or scoffed at the faith of the masses of our people."

At his first inauguration, McKinley took the oath of office, then kissed the Bible which was opened to this passage: "Give me now wisdom and knowledge, that I may go out and come in before this people: for who can judge this thy people, that is so great?" (2 Chron. 1:10).

Abraham Lincoln, a greatly loved president, was never demonstrative about prayer, but his words and the observations of many who knew him, lead us to know that he was a man of prayer. Lincoln's private secretary John Nicolay, for example, observed, "Mr. Lincoln was a praying man. I know that to be a fact...." Once, when Lincoln was before a group of clergymen, one of the ministers expressed the hope that God was on "our side" (the side of the Union during the War Between the States). The president's response has been recorded for posterity, "I don't agree with you. I am not at all concerned about that, for I know that the Lord is *always* on the side of the *right*. But it is my constant anxiety and prayer that I and the *nation* should be on the Lord's side."

Many have wondered if Jefferson was a man of prayer. It is clear that he spent much time thinking and studying about God and prayer. The fact is that he spent many of his evenings in the White House writing down the teachings of Jesus that held great importance to him.

Eventually this compilation came to be known as *The Jefferson Bible*. As regards prayer, Jefferson once stated, "I have sworn upon the altar of God eternal hostility against every form of tyranny over the mind of man."

John Adams, one of the most religious of all our presidents, wrote, "Does not natural morality, and much more Christian benevolence, make it our indispensible duty to lay ourselves out, to serve our fellow creatures to the utmost of our power...?" His wife, Abigail, reflected her husband's belief when she wrote to a friend, "A patriot without religion in my estimation is as great a paradox as an honest man without the fear of God....The Scriptures tell us righteousness exalteth a nation."

President John F. Kennedy lent credence to Abigail's assertion when he wrote, "While they came from a wide variety of religious backgrounds and held a wide variety of religious beliefs, each of our presidents in his own way has placed a special trust in God. Those who were strongest intellectually were also strongest spiritually."

It is gratifying to note that each of our presidents has had the wisdom to realize that their office is a sacred trust. The prayers of God's people throughout the centuries and in every corner of our land have helped our presidents to hold onto this perception. It is imperative for each one of us to continue to hold our leaders in prayer. Paul's urgent admonition to Timothy is an exhortation for us today: "I exhort therefore, that, *first of all,* supplications, prayers, intercessions, and giving of thanks, be made for all men; For kings, and for all that are in authority; that we may lead a quiet and peaceable life in all godliness and honesty" (1 Tim. 2:1-2, italics mine).

More than an exhortation, this verse of sacred Scripture is a vital prayer promise. If we pray for our leaders with diligence and commitment, we will be able to lead a quiet and peaceable life in all godliness and honesty.

It may well be that our presidents know the importance of prayer even better than the rest of us because of the pressures and crises they are called upon to face. An article by Hugh Sidey in the summer, 1967, issue of *Life* magazine, reveals how this works:

> *The men who have served in the Presidency have often found that their faiths, perhaps implanted years before and allowed to become dormant, take on new meaning once they gain the Oval Office. Great national crises, of course, produce the most profound religious experiences. . . . The apocalyptic power given Presidents in the nuclear age may have deepened their religious feeling; having godlike powers of destruction in their hands may have made them more conscious of human limitations. Under these stirrings they come often to feel that conventional forms of worship are inadequate and irrelevant, and dig deep inside themselves to revivify their own religious promptings.*

Righteousness exalteth a nation: but sin is a reproach to any people. (Prov. 13:34)

CALL TO INTERCESSION

And I sought for a man among them, that should make up the hedge, and stand in the gap before me for the land, that I should not destroy it; but I found none. (Ezek. 22:30)

Intercessors for Our Country

God is searching our land for intercessors — people who will combine the principles and promises of His Word with powerful prayer — in behalf of our land and its people.

Because *Prayers That Prevail for America* is in your hands it is likely that God is calling you to help to "make up the hedge and stand in the gap before Him" in behalf of the United States of America. What a privilege! What a ministry! This is an area where you can serve your God and your country in a vitally important way.

Unless we earnestly and faithfully beseech the Lord in behalf of our land, the Scriptures warn that God's strong hand of judgment will fall against our nation. This book was written with this sobering truth in mind. It is an intercession/warfare manual to help believers enter into effective prayer and intercession. Its Bible-based, topical prayers are promise-packed guidelines for praying God's Word with power and purpose in behalf of our land, its leaders, its people, its problems and all those we care about.

God listened to Abraham's intercessory prayers in behalf of Sodom and Gomorrha, and because of this, the righteous citizens escaped God's judgment fires. This same principle applies to us today:

> *If my people, which are called by my name,*
> *shall humble themselves, and pray, and seek my*
> *face, and turn from their wicked ways; then will*
> *I hear from heaven, and will forgive their sin,*
> *and will heal their land. (2 Chron. 7:14)*

The prayers of godly people in the United States are the strong thread that holds the United States together. Because we have been "one nation under God" for more than two centuries, we continue to enjoy God's blessings and the individual liberties we hold so dear. Godly people who know the value of earnest prayer are the backbone of our nation.

God loves America. He loves the people of our land. At the same time, however, He hates our sins and immorality. The call to intercessors today is to "Fight the good fight of faith, lay hold on eternal life, whereunto thou art also called, and hast professed a good profession before many witnesses" (1 Tim. 6:12).

This kind of spiritual warfare (the "good fight of faith") is waged, to a large degree, through prayer. Saint Paul revealed this truth in his letter to the Ephesians:

> *Finally, my brethren, be strong in the Lord,*
> *and in the power of his might. Put on the whole*
> *armor of God, that ye may be able to stand*

against the wiles of the devl. For we wrestle not against flesh and blood, but against principalities, against powers, against the rulers of the darkness of this world, against spiritual wickedness in high places. Wherefore take unto you the whole armour of God, that ye may be able to withstand in the evil day, and having done all, to stand. Stand therefore, having your loins girt about with truth, and having on the breastplate of righteousness; And your feet shod with the preparation of the gospel of peace; Above all, taking the shield of faith, wherewith ye shall be able to quench all the fiery darts of the wicked. And take the helmet of salvation, and the sword of the Spirit, which is the word of God; **Praying always with all prayer and supplication in the Spirit, and watching thereunto with all perseverance and supplication for all saints.** *(Eph. 6:10-18, emphasis mine)*

Though a fine distinction must be made between intercessory prayer and spiritual warfare, the Great Apostle makes it clear that all effective intercession must involve spiritual warfare. It also involves key attitudes and actions that prepare us to do battle.

The Armor of God

In order to become effective intercessors who rise to God's challenge for this hour, we need to be certain that we are well-equipped. *Prayers That Prevail for America* focuses on the preparation and equipment we need to be able to reach God's heart in behalf of others. The following components of intercessory prayer are based on Ephesians 6:10-18. These seven qualities and tools equip the prayer warrior for victory:

1. *The Power of God's Might.* Saint Luke reveals the source of the dynamic power that enables us to prevail in prayer:

> *But ye shall receive power, after that the Holy Ghost is come upon you: and ye shall be witnesses unto me both in Jerusalem, and in all Judaea, and in Samaria, and unto the uttermost part of the earth. (Acts 1:8)*

The power of God's Spirit who dwells within us makes us strong in the Lord and in the power of His might. The power to be a witness for our Lord is the same power that accomplishes great things for God through prayer.

2. *The Power of Truth.* We are commanded to gird our loins with truth. All guile, hypocrisy, deception and sin vanishes in the light of God's truth. Jesus said:

> *And ye shall know the truth, and the truth shall make you free. (John 8:32)*

As we speak the truth to God in prayer, fortified by the truths of His Word, we will see greater freedom coming to our nation and many will be set free from their bondages. Truth is one of the golden values that many have forgotten. The loss of truth brings darkness to an individual and a nation.

3. *The Breastplate of Righteousness.* No deception, sin, fear or failure can penetrate our spirits if we put on the protective gear of righteousness. Like a bullet-proof vest, righteousness blocks all the attempts of the evil one

to destroy our faith, and his goals to cause our nation to fall are completely thwarted by God's righteousness.

Righteousness means right-standing with God. He gives us His righteousness as a free gift. This free gift of righteousness becomes ours when we believe in Jesus Christ through faith.

Jesus said:

> *But seek ye first the kingdom of God, and his righteousness; and all these things shall be added unto you. (Matt. 6:33)*

We seek God's kingdom and His righteousness through obedience and prayer. It is prayer that will usher in His kingdom throughout our land and it is praying God's Word that will enable us to appropriate His righteousness for ourselves and others.

"Righteousness exalteth a nation: but sin is a reproach to any people" (Prov. 14:34).

4. *The Preparation of the Gospel of Peace.* The shoes we wear as God's intercessors are sturdy and comfortable. They enable us to walk in the principles of God's Word. They lead us to share the good news with others. As the hearts of men and women and young people are transformed by the Gospel of Peace, change will come to our land. This needs to be the major concern of our intercession — God, send revival, and let it begin with me! Jesus said:

> *Let your light so shine before men, that they may see your good works, and glorify your Father which is in heaven. (Matt. 5:16)*

5. *The Shield of Faith.* During the Middle Ages, the knights who ventured forth on the Crusades strapped bucklers (metal shields) to their forearms so that they would be prepared to deflect the arrows and spears of their enemies. Our buckler as intercessors serves the same purpose:

> *For by thee I have run through a troop: by my God have I leaped over a wall. As for God, his way is perfect; the word of the Lord is tried: he is a buckler to all them that trust in him. (2 Sam. 22:30-31)*

God is our buckler. As we learn how to incorporate His Word into our intercessions, we will be enabled to run through a troop and leap over a wall. The Word of God imparts faith to its listeners, and faith appropriates God's promises for our land. Lord, grant us hearing ears to hear your words and have hearts filled with faith.

6. *The Helmet of Salvation.* Learning to meditate upon God's Word and incorporating His promises into our prayers protects our minds like a helmet from all assaults and distractions. Our minds are renewed and transformed by the Bible:

> *. . . Christ also loved the church, and gave himself for it; That he might sanctify and cleanse it with the **washing of water by the word.** (Eph. 5:25-26, emphasis mine)*

Prayers That Prevail for America leads us into a deeper meditation of the Word of God and this equips us for victorious intercession, fruitfulness and prosperity. (See Psalms 1.)

7. *The Sword of the Spirit.* Our mighty weapon is the Holy Bible, the living Word of God. Jesus used the Word to overcome temptation, and we must follow His example. Through the Word of God we receive spiritual discernment and even the motives of our own hearts are revealed. Hear the Word of the Lord:

> *For the word of God is quick, and powerful, and sharper than any two-edged sword, piercing even to the dividing asunder of soul and spirit, and of the joints and marrow, and is a discerner of the thoughts and intents of the heart. (Heb. 4:12)*

The Sword of the Spirit (God's Word) always effects changes in the individual heart and it has the power to transform a nation. The Bible imparts faith to its readers. As we pray, we must stand with the Sword of the Lord poised for battle. Without Bibles in our public schools, it is not surprising to see many students and teachers without hope, the victims of Satan's schemes in our society today. No Bible, no truth. No Bible, no life. No Bible, no hope. No Bible, no wisdom.

It is the power of God's Word that forms the basis for the intercessory prayer ministry of our Lord Jesus Christ who is praying for you even as you read this book:

> *Neither is there any creature that is not manifest in his sight: but all things are naked and opened unto the eyes of him with whom we have to do. Seeing then that we have a great high priest, that is passed into the heavens, Jesus the Son of God, let us hold fast our profession. For we have not an high priest which cannot be*

touched with the feeling of our infirmities; but was in all points tempted like as we are, yet without sin. **Let us therefore come boldly before the throne of grace, that we may obtain mercy, and find grace to help in time of need.** *(Heb. 4:13-16, emphasis mine)*

God himself invites us to come boldly before His throne. We are able to do so when we stand firmly upon His Word. The greatest example of intercessory prayer is given to us by our Lord Jesus who prays continually for us. As we learn to pray according to His Word, His power is unleashed and we will find grace to help in time of need — grace for our own lives, our loved ones and our nation.

Each piece of God's armor is to be put on *daily with prayer.* Prayer keeps the armor glowing with the light of God's love and presence, and prayer keeps it strong so that no fiery darts of the wicked can penetrate our hearts.

Meditate on God's Word

Blessed is the man that walketh not in the counsel of the ungodly, nor standeth in the way of sinners, nor sitteth in the seat of the scornful. **But his delight is in the law of the Lord; and in his law doth he meditate day and night.** *And he shall be like a tree planted by the rivers of water, that bringeth forth his fruit in his season; his leaf also shall not wither; and whatsoever he doeth shall prosper. (Ps. 1:1-3, emphasis mine)*

The prayers in this book come directly from the Law of the Lord. They are meditational in that they are designed to help us think God's thoughts, understand His ways and reflect on His purposes in our intercession for our country and our fellow-citizens. In and of itself, such meditation is a process of spiritual renewal. Beyond that, it is therapeutic for our minds, souls and bodies. Above all, however, it is the springboard from which we can dive into the power and glory of intercessory prayer.

It is certain that many circumstances cannot be changed, except by prayer. People do not change unless they learn to yield to the Lord as a result of prayers of others who diligently beseech God for their salvation. Prayer can change our hearts, our loved ones, our society.

As we meditate on the truths and promises of the Bible, our attitudes, thoughts and behaviors change. We are cleansed from within and we are empowered to do battle in behalf of our Lord and the land we love. The results of this kind of dynamic meditation are profoundly liberating:

1. We become fruitful in all our endeavors, including prayer.
2. We become planted next to the River of Life, a powerful and refreshing stream that emanates from the throne of God and brings His sacred promises to us.
3. We experience prosperity in whatever we do, including prayer.

The principles outlined in this book are God's. As you incorporate them into your life of intercession, your prayers will become fruitful and powerful and prosperous.

Your life will be changed as your prayers bring results in others' lives and our nation at large.

God's Word on Intercession

The Scriptures, both Old and New Testaments, abound with exhortations, commands and examples related to intercessory prayer. Some pertinent passages are cited in the following paragraphs for your edification and understanding.

> *Yet it pleased the Lord to bruise him; he hath put him to grief: when thou shalt make his soul an offering for sin, he shall see his seed, he shall prolong his days, and the pleasure of the Lord shall prosper in his hand. He shall see of the travail of his soul, and shall be satisfied: by his knowledge shall my righteous servant justify many; for he shall bear their iniquities. Therefore will I divide him a portion with the great, and he shall divide the spoil with the strong; because he hath poured out his soul unto death: and he was numbered with the transgressors; and he bare the sin of many, **and made intercession for the transgressors.** (Isa. 53:10-12, emphasis mine)*

The very life and death of Jesus are intercessory prayers for us. By dying for us, He interceded in our behalf before God, our heavenly Father. And as He prayed for us on earth (see John 17:20-22), He continues to intercede for us before the Father's throne:

> *Wherefore he is able also to save them to the uttermost that come unto God by him, seeing*

he ever liveth to make intercession for them.
(Heb. 7:25, emphasis mine)

Through His death, Jesus showed us the importance of praying for transgressors. By way of example, therefore, He is asking us to pray for the transgressors of our land. "Greater love hath no man than this, that a man lay down his life for his friends" (John 15:13).

The Prophet Jeremiah reveals the importance of utilizing the Word of God in our intercessory praying:

But if they be prophets, and if the word of the Lord be with them, let them now make intercession to the Lord of hosts. (Jer. 27:18, emphasis mine)

God is calling us to intercession, but He wants us to be certain that His Word is with us as we pray. His Word brings life, power and faith to our prayers.

We must always remember that we are not alone when we make intercession for America. There is a band of faithful believers who stand with us, both in this country and abroad. Jesus prays with us as well, and another member of the blessed Trinity empowers us in our intercessions:

Likewise the Spirit also helpeth our infirmities: for we know not what we should pray for as we ought: but the Spirit itself maketh intercession for us with groanings which cannot be uttered. And he that searcheth the hearts knoweth what is the mind of the Spirit, because he maketh intercession for the saints according to the will of God. (Rom. 8:26, emphasis mine)

God's Holy Spirit guides us in our intercession through the Bible and through the "still, small voice" that speaks to our spirits. The Spirit of God is praying for us, with us and through us!

It is dynamically exciting to realize that the ministry of intercessory prayer invites the power of God's Spirit into our lives and through this process, we join hands in prayer with our Lord Jesus Christ:

> *Who is he that condemneth? It is Christ that died, yea rather, that is risen again, who is even at the right hand of God, **who also maketh intercession for us.** (Rom. 8:34, emphasis mine).*

Praying for a Nation

Is it biblical to pray for a country in the same way that we might intercede for an individual, a church or a group of people? The Old Testament and the New Testament give numerous affirmative answers to this question both through precept and example.

In Romans, Paul reminds us of the story of Elijah who made intercession against Israel:

> *Lord, they have killed thy prophets, and digged down thine altars; and I am left alone, and they seek my life. (Rom. 11:3)*

Elijah must have been surprised by the Lord's answer:

> *I have reserved to myself seven thousand men, who have not bowed the knee to the image of Baal. (Rom. 11:4)*

The Lord was moved by Elijah's intercession. He knew how the prophet felt, but He would not come against

Israel, despite their idolatry, because He knew there was a remnant of 7,000 faithful men who had not bowed their knees to Baal.

There is a message of hope in this story for the righteous and faithful Christians of our nation too. Surely there are more than 7,000 in America who have not bowed their knees to other gods.

Paul prayed for Israel, asking God to save the Hebrew people:

> *Brethren, my heart's desire and prayer to God for Israel is, that they might be saved. (Rom. 10:1)*

This positive attitude of caring and concern is essential in all our intercessory praying. As Jesus is touched with our infirmities, so must our hearts be moved with regard to the needs of a nation or a person for whom we are praying. Jesus wept over Jerusalem as He prayed for them. Jeremiah became known as "the weeping prophet" because his empathy for the people brought him to tears as he prayed for them. It was Paul's "heart's desire" to see the salvation of Israel.

Another essential component of effective intercession is identification. As God enables us to identify with the people of our nation and their needs, we find ourselves being humbled before God. True humility leads us to see ourselves and others as God sees us — a people in need of His mercy and power. A people whose righteousness is in Christ alone.

The prophet Daniel displayed this identification and humility when he prayed for his people:

*And I prayed unto the Lord my God, and
made my confession, and said, O Lord, the great
and dreadful God, keeping the covenant and
mercy to them that love him, and to them that
keep his commandments; We have sinned, and
have committed iniquity, and have done
wickedly, and have rebelled, even by departing
from thy precepts and from thy judgments:
Neither have we hearkened unto thy servants the
prophets, which spake in thy name to our kings,
our princes, and our fathers, and to all the
people of the land. O Lord, righteousness
belongeth unto thee, but unto us confusion of
faces, as at this day; to the men of Judah, and
to the inhabitants of Jerusalem, and unto all
Israel, that are near, and that are far off,
through all the countries whither thou hast driven
them, because of their trespass that they have
trespassed against thee. (Dan. 9:4-7)*

As we pray for the United States of America we need
to let God break our hearts with the same things that break
His heart, never forgetting to love deeply the people of
our country even though some may be involved in gross
sins and immorality. The nation will be reached if the godly
remain faithful prayer warriors who walk in love and
humility before the people.

*Let the priests, the ministers of the Lord,
weep between the porch and the altar, and let
them say, Spare thy people, O Lord, and give
not thine heritage to reproach, that the heathen*

should rule over them: wherefore should they say among the people, Where is their God? (Joel 2:17)

Let us make the prophet's prayer the prayer of our hearts for America today: "Lord, spare your people. Give not the heritage of our nation to reproach so that the heathen would be able to rule over us. May your church in our land be so strong that people everywhere would become aware of your purpose."

This prayer, paraphrased from the Bible, provides the reader with a taste of the style of the topical prayers found in this book. God always accompanies His Word, and as we draw near to Him in faith, He draws near to us. (See James 4:8.) As we intercede for our nation, guided by God's Word and His Spirit, His gracious promise to His people will be fulfilled:

So shall my word be that goeth forth out of my mouth: it shall not return unto me void, but it shall accomplish that which I please, and it shall prosper in the thing whereto I sent it. (Isa. 55:11)

What a privilege it is to serve the Lord in the vital ministry of intercession. As Andrew Murray points out, "Like Him [Christ], give yourself to God as a sacrifice for men: it is your highest nobility; it is your true and full union to Him. It will be to you, as to Him, your power of intercession. Beloved Christian! Come and give your whole heart and life to intercession, and you will know its blessedness and power. God asks nothing less. The world needs nothing less. Christ asks nothing less. Let nothing less be what we offer to God." (From *The Ministry of Intercession* by Andrew Murray.)

ACTIVE INTERCESSION

I have set watchmen upon thy walls, O Jerusalem, which shall never hold their peace day nor night: ye that make mention of the Lord, keep not silence, And give Him no rest . . . till he make Jerusalem a praise in the earth. (Isa. 62:6-7)

In the epigram above Isaiah reveals a key component of effective intercession — perseverance. As one God has called to be an intercessor for America, you are a watchman on the walls of our nation. Our mission is clear: to fervently pray, night and day, till God makes America a praise in the earth.

A helpful acronym may be used as a framework on which to build your prayers of intercession. It is formed from the letters found in the word "active." The letters are used as the first initials in six essential components of effective intercession as follows:

A — Adoration
C — Confession
T — Thanksgiving
I — Intercession
V — Verification
E — Expectancy

Active involvement in the ministry of intercession requires all six ingredients. Let's look carefully at what the Bible has to say about these aspects of prayer so that we will become better equipped to take our "stand in the gap" for our country.

Adoration

Through worship, we are able to enter the Holy of Holies where we approach God's throne with reverence and with confidence. As the Psalmist revealed, we are to "Enter into his gates with thanksgiving, and into his courts with praise: be thankful unto him, and bless his name" (Ps. 100:4).

Worship, praise and thanksgiving enable us to adore the Lord in all His glory, to thank Him for all He has done and will do, and most importantly, to thank Him for who He is — the Almighty God who is able to intervene in the affairs of our nation with awesome and eternal results!

> *O come, let us adore Him,*
> *O come, let us adore Him,*
> *O come, let us adore Him,*
> *Christ, the Lord.*

As we learn to focus on the Lord instead of the problems of our nation, we soon experience that wonderful peace that enables us to transcend the difficulties of life and go to the Source of all that is good.

Turn your eyes upon Jesus,
Look full in His wonderful face,
And the things of earth will grow strangely dim,
In the light of His glory and grace.

This is what adoration can do for us, and it sets the stage for God's miracle-working power to be revealed in the situations and lives for which we are making intercession. Active intercession, therefore, begins with a settling down into the rest that God promises to all who are heavy-laden: "Come unto me, all ye that labour and are heavy laden, and I will give you rest. Take my yoke upon you, and learn of me; for I am meek and lowly in heart: and ye shall find rest unto your souls. For my yoke is easy, and my burden is light" (Matt. 11:28-30).

This is the "better part" that was chosen by Mary when she sat at the footstool of our Lord. Her sister, Martha, resented Mary's choice, but Jesus gently rebuked her: "Martha, Martha, thou art careful and troubled about many things; But one thing is needful: and Mary hath chosen that good part, which shall not be taken away from her" (Luke 10:41-42).

At the footstool of Jesus, Mary was involved in the "one needful thing" — adoring her Master and building upon her relationship with Him. All effective intercession begins the same way, as we find that "place of quiet rest, near to the heart of God. A place where sin cannot molest, near to the heart of God." We adore the Lord for His magnificence, His splendor, His glory, His power, His love and His willingness to give so much in answer to our prayers. What a great God He is!

The writer of the Book of Hebrews clarifies our insight into the way a worshipful sense of adoration permits us to intercede and make supplication in behalf of others:

Let us therefore come boldly unto the throne of grace, that we may obtain mercy, and find grace to help in time of need. (Heb. 4:16)

America is facing a time of great need in the present hour. Through intercession, we can obtain mercy and find grace to help our nation and its people. As we approach God's throne, however, we can do so boldly and confidently, but only if we take the time to adore and revere the God of glory.

Andrew Murray puts it well, "The things that are impossible with men are possible with God. When we think of the great things we ask for, how impossible they seem in the light of our insignificance. Prayer is not only wishing or asking, but believing and accepting. Be still before God, and ask Him to let you know Him as the Almighty One. Leave your petitions with Him who works wonders." (From *The Ministry of Intercession* by Andrew Murray.)

Confession

In the Lord's Prayer, Jesus begins with adoration: "Our Father which art in heaven, Hallowed be thy name." He also incorporates the component of confession in His model prayer: "And forgive us our sins; for we also forgive every one that is indebted to us" (Luke 11:4). Did you ever notice that Jesus' prayer was primarily one of intercession? He prays not only for himself, but for others:

"*Our* Father which art in heaven" (Luke 11:2).

"Give *us* day by day *our* daily bread" (Luke 11:3).

"And forgive *us our* sins; for *we* also forgive *every one* that is indebted to us" (Luke 11:4).

"And lead *us* not into temptation; but deliver *us* from evil" (Luke 11:4).

The greatest part of the Master's prayer life was devoted to intercession for others, as we see reflected in His great prayer for unity in John 17:

I pray for them: I pray not for the world, but for them which thou hast given me; for they are thine. (John 17:9)

Hallelujah! He continues to make intercession for us. Because He does, we are able to confess our sins with full knowledge that God will forgive us if we truly repent. This is made possible for us because Jesus is our Advocate, continually pleading our cause before our Father in heaven.

If we confess our sins, he is faithful and just to forgive us our sins, and to cleanse us from all unrighteousness. (1 John 1:9)

For there is one God, and one mediator between God and men, the man Christ Jesus; Who gave himself a ransom for all. (1 Tim. 2:5-6)

My little children, these, things write I unto you, that ye sin not. And if any man sin, we have an advocate with the Father, Jesus Christ the righteous: And he is the propitiation for our sins: and not for ours only, but also for the sins of the whole world. (1 John 2:1-2)

Why should confession be a part of our intercessory praying? Sometimes in our intercession in behalf of the Church and our nation, we may find that there is a need for collective confession of sins of omission and commission. We may need to confess a general sin of prayerlessness, for example, in behalf of the Body of

Christ. Or the sin of materialism in the Church or the nation.

There is also a need for personal confession at the outset of our intercessions. Sin separates us from God and from our fellow-believers. Confession restores those relationships and brings forgiveness. The Psalmist wrote, "If I regard iniquity in my heart, the Lord will not hear me" (Ps. 66:18).

Thanksgiving

Certainly, the most appropriate response to being forgiven is thanksgiving. A thankful heart opens up to all God has in store for it. Paul wrote, "Rejoice evermore. Pray without ceasing. In every thing give thanks: for this is the will of God in Christ Jesus concerning you" (1 Thess. 5:16-18).

What is God's will for you? To rejoice, to pray without ceasing and to give thanks in everything. Yes, we are to give thanks in intercession as well — thanks for all God has done, what He will do and who He is.

There is an important relationship between thanksgiving and joy. A thankful heart is a joyful heart. Joy and thanksgiving are vital components in our intercessory praying.

> *Behold, I will do a new thing; now it shall spring forth; shall ye not know it? I will even make a way in the wilderness, and rivers in the desert. The beast of the field shall honour me, the dragons and the owls: because I give waters in the wilderness, and rivers in the desert, to give*

*drink to my people, my chosen. This people have
I formed for myself; they shall shew forth my
praise. (Isa. 43:19-21)*

Through intercessory prayers for our nation we will
be able to watch God do something new in our midst. His
waters of life will flow in the wasteland and His people
will show forth His praise.

The promise of intercession fills our hearts with
praise. Just to know that God made us for himself causes
our hearts to be thankful. Jesus said, "Verily, verily, I
say unto you, Whatsoever ye shall ask the Father in my
name, *he will give it you.* Hitherto have ye asked nothing
in my name: ask, and ye shall receive, *that your joy may
be full*" (John 16:23-24, italics mine).

Intercession

Hear the Word of the Lord:

*And he saw that there was no man, and
wondered that there was no intercessor. (Isa.
59:16)*

*God forbid that I should sin against the
Lord in ceasing to pray for you. (1 Sam. 12:23)*

*What things soever ye desire, when ye pray,
believe that ye receive them, and ye shall have
them. (Mark 11:24)*

*I will pour upon the house of David... the
spirit of grace and of supplications. (Zech.
12:10)*

Praying always with all prayer and supplication in the Spirit, and watching thereunto with all perseverance and supplication for all the saints. (Eph. 6:18)

The above are some of the Scriptures that relate to intercessory prayer. There are several others as well, and there are numerous examples of believers engaged in this vital ministry in the Bible. For example, the Psalmist prayed, "Wilt thou not revive us again: that thy people may rejoice in thee? (Ps. 85:6). And Habakkuk also sought the Lord for revival, "O Lord, revive thy work in the midst of the years" (Hab. 3:2).

The New Testament is strengthened by the intercessory prayers of Jesus, His disciples and His apostles.

The Bible is clear in its prescription of intercession as the antidote for the troubles faced by believers and the world. We are given examples of intercession in behalf of the world, the Church, specific believers, ungodly individuals, rulers, nations, cities and the future. As Paul pointed out to Timothy, these scriptural examples are for our admonition:

All scripture is given by inspiration of God, and is profitable for doctrine, for reproof, for correction, for instruction in righteousness: That the man of God may be perfect, throughly furnished unto all good works. (2 Tim. 3:16-17)

The fact is, we are commanded to pray for one another, for all men, for rulers, for the Church, for the world and for the future. In First Timothy we read:

> *I exhort therefore, that, first of all,*
> *supplications, prayers, intercessions, and giving*
> *of thanks, be made for all men; For kings, and*
> *for all that are in authority; that we may lead*
> *a quiet and peaceable life in all godliness and*
> *honesty. For this is good and acceptable in the*
> *sight of God our Saviour; Who will have all men*
> *to be saved, and to come unto the knowledge of*
> *the truth. (1 Tim. 2:1-4)*

The Apostle Paul classifies and divides the ministry of intercession into four categories:

1. Supplications.

2. Prayers.

3. Intercessions.

4. The giving of thanks.

Each of these is to be an heart-felt expression in behalf of others. Though each component is closely related, there are fine distinctions of emphases represented by each.

Supplications are prayers that focus on specific needs. Personal supplications, for example, are prayers that request God to provide something that is needed or to intervene in specific situations. All intercessions involve supplications, but not all supplications are intercessory in nature.

The root of supplications implies the attitude of humility. The supplicant's stance is one of utter destitution, poverty of spirit, that leads him to humbly entreat God for that which he cannot supply for himself or others. This dependence on God is integral to all effective praying, particularly the prayer of intercession. We must always remember the words of Jesus: "Without me ye can do nothing" (John 15:5).

Prayers are intimate conversations with our Lord, our Father, our Master, our Friend. They involve listening as well as speaking. They also involve waiting. As David E. Rosage points out, "Since prayer is a communication between God and ourselves, and since what God has to say is far more important than what we have to talk over with Him, then the first requisite for prayer is that we learn to listen." (From *Speak, Lord, Your Servant Is Listening*.) Jesus said, "My sheep hear my voice, and I know them, and they follow me" (John 10:27).

Intercessions are, according to Webster, "prayers, petitions or entreaties in favor of another." In effect, when we make intercession for others, we are standing in proxy for them before God. We humbly beseech God for their needs. We plead their case before His throne. We bear their burdens. We cry their tears. We thank God in their behalf, and we seek His forgiveness for their sins. We do this because they can't or won't or simply don't know their need. God knows and He loves them. Therefore, He listens when we bring their names and needs to Him.

When we pray for fellow-believers, we do so in order to strengthen them spiritually, to fight their battles with them and to fulfill the Father's plan and purpose for us.

The giving of thanks is an appropriate aspect of all prayers, whether they be personal or intercessory in nature. The Father heart of God is greatly stirred when His children express gratitude to Him for His care, His goodness and His providence in their lives.

Paul gives great priority to the life of prayer and intercession. He writes, "I exhort, therefore, that, *first of all*, supplications, prayers, intercessions, and giving of thanks, be made for all men" (1 Tim. 2:1, italics mine).

Further, he exhorts us to intercede for *all men,* including "kings, and for all that are in authority" (1 Tim. 2:2). If we obey this exhortation faithfully, the result will be that we will be able to "lead a quiet and peaceable life in all godliness and honesty" (1 Tim. 2:2).

The Great Apostle goes on to establish a clear link between intercession and revival. God wants " all men to be saved, and to come unto the knowledge of the truth" (1 Tim. 2:4). He makes it clear that a major part of our intercessions should be aimed at the lost who need a Savior.

In view of this, many of the topical prayers in this book are intercessions from the Word of God in behalf of those in authority, our fellow-believers and the unsaved.

Verification

There are several ways in which we can verify the effects and power of our intercessions. First and foremost, we must always make sure that our prayers are in line with the Word of God. In this way, we can always be certain that we are praying in accord with the will of God because we know that His entire counsel to us is revealed in the Bible. (See our earlier work, *Prayers That Prevail — The Believer's Manual of Prayers*, for further insights into the dynamic that is unleashed when believers pray the Word of God.)

By keeping a prayer journal, we can actually record the miraculous results of our intercessions. This, in turn, builds our faith and propels us into deeper ministries of intercession. Few ministries are as powerful and exciting as that of intercession. God delights in answering the prayers of His people.

When the Apostle Peter was in prison, his fellow-believers interceded in his behalf before the Throne of Grace. He was released miraculously, but his friends found it so hard to believe that their prayers had been answered so dramatically.

> *And as Peter knocked at the door of the gate, a damsel came to hearken, named Rhoda. And when she knew Peter's voice, she opened not the gate for gladness, but ran in, and told how Peter stood before the gate. And they said unto her, Thou art mad. But she constantly affirmed that it was even so. Then said they, It is his angel. But Peter continued knocking: and when they had opened the door, and saw him, they were astonished. (Acts 12:13-16)*

This was a case where God responded to intercessory prayer even when those who prayed had little faith that He would answer. Imagine what will happen when we pray for our nation with the full faith that God's Word imparts to our hearts.

James wrote, "Ye ask, and receive not, because ye ask amiss, that ye may consume it upon your lusts" (James 4:3). Earlier, he had advised, "Ask in faith, nothing wavering. For he that wavereth is like a wave of the sea driven with the wind and tossed. Let not that man think that he shall receive any thing of the Lord" (James 1:6-7).

This leads us to our last component of active intercession — EXPECTATION.

Expectation

The secret of effective intercession is found in the five-letter word, FAITH. Jesus declared, "What things soever ye desire, when ye pray, *believe* that ye receive them, and ye shall have them" (Mark 11:24, italics mine).

Faith comes from the Word of God. Paul wrote, "So then faith cometh by hearing, and hearing by the word of God" (Rom. 10:17). By incorporating the truths of the Bible into our ministry of intercession, our own faith is strengthened and we are able to reach out in full expectation that God will indeed answer our prayers. Jesus said that this is an absolute necessity for a life of prevailing prayer.

Andrew Murray wrote, "The receiving from God in faith — the believing acceptance of the answer with the perfect, praising assurance that it has been given — is not necessarily the experience or subjective possession of the gift we have asked for. At times, there may be a long interval of time between our asking and our actually receiving. In other cases, the believing supplicant may immediately experience the actual enjoyment of what he has received. It is especially in the former case that we need to have faith and patience: faith to rejoice in the assurance of the answer bestowed and received, and to begin acting on that answer even though nothing is felt; patience to wait if, for the present, there is no sensible proof of its reality. We can count on it: *Ye shall have,* in tangible reality." (From *The Ministry of Intercession* by Andrew Murray.)

Expect God to fulfill His will in answer to your prayers. *Expect* Him to intervene in the situations that concern you. *Expect* Him to hear you, to share your deepest concerns, to act in response to your cries. *Expect* Him to heal our land, to bring revival to our nation.

> *Ask, and it shall be given you; seek, and ye shall find; knock, and it shall be opened unto you: For every one that asketh receiveth; and he that seeketh findeth; and to him that knocketh it shall be opened. Or what man is there of you, whom if his son ask bread, will he give him a stone? Or if he ask a fish, will he give him a serpent? If ye then, being evil, know how to give good gifts unto your children, how much more shall your Father which is in heaven give good things to them that ask him? (Matt. 7:7-11)*

Intercession — not a passive, weak undertaking, but an active participation in the fulfillment of God's will on earth! Remember God's servant Job? He had lost his family, his possessions, his health, his friends. Even so, the Lord blessed the end of Job's life more than the beginning. As a matter of fact, the Lord gave Job two times more than what he had previously. What was the key to such blessing?

> *And the Lord turned the captivity of Job, **when he prayed for his friends:** also the Lord gave Job twice as much as he had before. (Job 42:10, emphasis mine)*

The full power of intercession has yet to be revealed to our nation, but once the Church learns the importance of active intercession in behalf of others, God's power will be unleashed in our land!

PRAYER PROMISES

(1)   The God of my rock; in him will I trust: he is my shield, and the horn of my salvation, my high tower, and my refuge, my saviour; thou savest me from violence. I will call on the Lord, who is worthy to be praised: so shall I be saved from mine enemies. (2 Sam. 22:3-4)

(2)   In my distress I called upon the Lord, and cried to my God: and he did hear my voice out of his temple, and my cry did enter into his ears. (2 Sam. 22:7)

(3)   Thus saith the Lord, the God of David thy father, I have heard thy prayer, I have seen thy tears: behold, I will heal thee. (2 Kings 20:5)

(4)   He heareth the cry of the afflicted. (Job 34:28)

(5)   But know that the Lord hath set apart him that is godly for himself: the Lord will hear when I call unto him. (Ps. 4:3)

(6)   He forgetteth not the cry of the humble. (Ps. 9:12)

(7)   Blessed be the Lord, because he hath heard the voice of my supplications. (Ps. 28:6)

(8)   I sought the Lord, and he heard me, and delivered me from all my fears. (Ps. 34:4)

(9)   They looked unto him, and were lightened: and their faces were not ashamed. (Ps. 34:5)

(10)   This poor man cried, and the Lord heard him, and saved him out of all his troubles. (Ps. 34:6)

(11)   Offer unto God thanksgiving; and pay thy vows unto the most High: And call upon me in the day of trouble: I will deliver thee, and thou shalt glorify me. (Ps. 50:14-15)

(12)   He shall call upon me, and I will answer him: I will be with him in trouble; I will deliver him, and honour him. With long life will I satisfy him, and shew him my salvation. (Ps. 91:15-16)

(13)   In my distress I cried unto the Lord, and he heard me. (Ps. 120:1)

(14)   The Lord is nigh unto all them that call upon him, to all that call upon him in truth. (Ps. 145:18)

(15)   The Lord is far from the wicked; but he heareth the prayer of the righteous. (Prov. 15:29)

(16)   Then shall ye call upon me, and ye shall go and pray unto me, and I will hearken unto you. And ye shall seek me, and find me, when ye shall search for me with all your heart. And I will be found of you, saith the Lord: and I will turn away your captivity, and I will gather you from all the nations. (Jer. 29:12-14)

(17)   Call unto me, and I will answer thee, and shew thee great and mighty things, which thou knowest not. (Jer. 33:3)

(18)   And it shall come to pass, that whosoever shall call on the name of the Lord shall be delivered. (Joel 2:32)

(19)   They shall call on my name, and I will hear them: I will say, It is my people: and they shall say, The Lord is my God. (Zech. 13:9)

(20)   Your Father knoweth what things ye have need of, before ye ask him. (Matt. 6:8)

(21)   Ask, and it shall be given you; seek, and ye shall find; knock, and it shall be opened unto you: For every one that asketh receiveth; and he that seeketh findeth; and to him that knocketh it shall be opened. (Matt. 7:7-8)

(22)   If ye then, being evil, know how to give good gifts unto your children, how much more shall your Father which is in heaven give good things to them that ask him? (Matt. 7:11)

(23)   Again I say unto you, That if two of you shall agree on earth as touching any thing that they shall ask, it shall be done for them of my Father which is in heaven. For where two or three are gathered together in my name, there am I in the midst of them. (Matt. 18:19-20)

(24)   And all things, whatsoever ye shall ask in prayer, believing, ye shall receive. (Matt. 21:22)

(25)   And Jesus answering saith unto them, Have faith in God. For verily I say unto you, That whosoever shall say unto this mountain, Be thou removed, and be thou cast into the sea; and shall not doubt in his heart, but shall believe that those things which he saith shall come to pass; he shall have whatsoever he saith. Therefore I say unto you, What things soever ye desire, when ye pray, believe that ye receive them, and ye shall have them. And when

ye stand praying, forgive, if ye have ought against any: that your Father also which is in heaven may forgive you your trespasses. (Mark 11:22-25)

(26)   Behold, I give unto you power to tread on serpents and scorpions, and over all the power of the enemy: and nothing shall by any means hurt you. (Luke 10:19)

(27)   But I know, that even now, whatsoever thou wilt ask of God, God will give it thee. (John 11:22)

(28)   And whatsoever ye shall ask in my name, that will I do, that the Father may be glorified in the Son. If ye shall ask any thing in my name, I will do it. (John 14:13-14)

(29)   If ye abide in me, and my words abide in you, ye shall ask what ye will, and it shall be done unto you. (John 15:7)

(30)   Verily, verily, I say unto you, Whatsoever ye shall ask the Father in my name, he will give it you. (John 16:23)

(31)   Hitherto have ye asked nothing in my name: ask, and ye shall receive, that your joy may be full. (John 16:24)

(32)   At that day ye shall ask in my name: and I say not unto you, that I will pray the Father for you: For the Father himself loveth you, because ye have loved me, and have believed that I came out from God. (John 16:26-27)

(33)   For there is no difference between the Jew and the Greek: for the same Lord over all is rich unto all that call upon him. (Rom. 10:12)

(34)   Now unto him that is able to do exceeding abundantly above all that we ask or think, according to the power that worketh in us, Unto him be glory in the church by Christ Jesus throughout all ages, world without end. Amen. (Eph. 3:20-21)

(35)   Be careful for nothing; but in every thing by prayer and supplication with thanksgiving let your requests be made known unto God. And the peace of God, which passeth all understanding, shall keep your hearts and minds through Christ Jesus. (Phil. 4:6-7)

(36)   Rejoice evermore. Pray without ceasing. In every thing give thanks: for this is the will of God in Christ Jesus concerning you. (1 Thess. 5:16-18)

(37)   Faithful is he that calleth you, who also will do it. (1 Thess. 5:24)

(38)   I exhort therefore, that, first of all, supplications, prayers, intercessions, and giving of thanks, be made for all men; For kings, and for all that are in authority; that we may lead a quiet and peaceable life in all godliness and honesty. For this is good and acceptable in the sight of God our Saviour. (1 Tim. 2:1-3)

(39)   I will therefore that men pray every where, lifting up holy hands, without wrath and doubting. (1 Tim. 2:8)

(40)   Let us therefore come boldly unto the throne of grace, that we may obtain mercy, and find grace to help in time of need. (Heb. 4:16)

(41)   But without faith it is impossible to please him: for he that cometh to God must believe that he is, and that he is a rewarder of them that diligently seek him. (Heb. 11:6)

(42)   If any of you lack wisdom, let him ask of God, that giveth to all men liberally, and upbraideth not; and it shall be given him. But let him ask in faith, nothing wavering. For he that wavereth is like a wave of the sea driven with the wind and tossed. (James 1:5-6)

(43)   Ye have not, because ye ask not. (James 4:2)

(44)   Ye ask, and receive not, because ye ask amiss. (James 4:3)

(45)   Submit yourselves therefore to God. Resist the devil, and he will flee from you. (James 4:7)

(46)   And the prayer of faith shall save the sick, and the Lord shall raise him up. (James 5:15)

(47)   Pray for one another, that ye may be healed. (James 5:16)

(48)   The effectual fervent prayer of a righteous man availeth much. (James 5:16)

(49)   For the eyes of the Lord are over the righteous, and his ears are open unto their prayers. (1 Pet. 3:12)

(50)   And whatsoever we ask, we receive of him, because we keep his commandments, and do those things that are pleasing in his sight. (1 John 3:22)

(51)   And this is the confidence that we have in him, that, if we ask any thing according to his will, he heareth us. (1 John 5:14)

(52)   And if we know that he hear us, whatsoever we ask, we know that we have the petitions that we desired of him. (1 John 5:15)

(53)   Now unto him that is able to keep you from falling, and to present you faultless before the presence of his glory with exceeding joy, To the only wise God our Saviour, be glory and majesty, dominion and power, both now and ever. Amen. (Jude 24-25)

(54)   Behold, I stand at the door, and knock: if any man hear my voice, and open the door, I will come in to him, and will sup with him, and he with me. (Rev. 3:20)

(55)   And the smoke of the incense, which came with the prayers of the saints, ascended up before God out of the angel's hand. (Rev. 8:4)

(56)   And they overcame him by the blood of the Lamb, and by the word of their testimony; and they loved not their lives unto the death. (Rev. 12:11)

For all the promises of God in him are yea,
and in him Amen, unto the glory of God by us.
(2 Cor. 1:20)

PRAYERS FOR AMERICA

I have set watchmen upon thy walls, O Jerusalem, which shall never hold their peace day nor night: ye that make mention of the Lord, keep not silence, And give him no rest, till he make Jerusalem a praise in the earth. (Isa. 62:6-7)

Abortion
(The Unborn Child)

Key Thought: Each unborn child is fearfully and wonderfully made.

Key Scripture: *"For you created my inmost being; you knit me together in my mother's womb. I praise you because I am fearfully and wonderfully made; your works are wonderful, I know that full well. My frame was not hidden from you when I was made in the secret place. When I was woven together in the depths of the earth, your eyes saw my unformed body. All the days ordained for me were written in your book before one of them came to be"* *(Ps. 139:13-16, NIV).*

Prayer: Heavenly Father, I thank you for the gift of children. Truly, they are an inheritance bequeathed to us by you, and the fruit of the womb is a reward you give to your people. As arrows are in the hand of a mighty man, so are the children you give to us. The happiest people are those who are blessed with children — they shall not be ashamed and they shall speak with the enemies in the gate.[1]

Lord, I am grieved and ashamed to know that so many abortions have occurred and are occurring in the United States. I know this grieves you too. Many people attempt to justify abortion as being a solution to several problems

65

that exist in our land today, but, God, you know our hearts. Almost always, that which is highly esteemed among men is an abomination in your sight. Lord, I know that abortion is an abomination in your sight[2] — a bitter stench in your nostrils.

When the ancient peoples sacrificed their infants to their idols, you intervened and brought judgment against these practices. When you observed idolaters killing innocent children, you warned the people that the wind would carry them all away. There is no peace, you pointed out, to the wicked.[3]

I pray for the unborn children of the world, Father, that their parents will take responsibility for these precious children whom you love and have created for special purposes. Lord Jesus, I thank you for your example of caring for children. You said that child-like faith is necessary to enter the Kingdom of heaven,[4] and that your Kingdom is open to children, for of such is your Kingdom made.[5] Thank you for watching out for the children of the world — both those who are born and those who are unborn.

Thank you, Jesus, for blessing the little children,[6] and for showing us how valuable these precious ones are. I beseech you, in behalf of the innocent unborn children of the world, to help those who favor abortion to understand the value of children to you, to repent of their sins and to humble themselves before you. Bring about a change in the values of Americans today, so that we may return to the family values that helped to make our nation strong.

As a Christian, I repent of the slaughter of our nation's unborn children, and I ask you to grant repentance to my fellow citizens as well.[7] Help each one of us take a stand to obey you rather than men,[8] because you, Father, raised up Jesus to grant us repentance[9] and give forgiveness of our sins. He who knew no sin became sin for us so that we might be made your righteousness in Him.[10] We have sinned, O God,[11] and it has not stopped. Have mercy on us. Have mercy on us. Have mercy on us.[12]

My earnest prayer is that you, Lord Jesus, would so move in the lives of our people that every knee should bow and that every tongue should confess that you are Lord to the glory of God the Father.[13] Only through such humility will people learn to trust in you with all their hearts, leaning not unto their own understanding, acknowledging you in all their ways so that you will direct their paths.[14] Draw many to you, Father, so that abortionists and those who favor abortion will turn from their wicked ways and save the lives of your children.[15]

Eternal God, you are our refuge, and underneath are your everlasting arms. Thank you for your promise that you will thrust out the enemy from before us.[16] There is no one like you because you are the shield of our help and the sword of our excellency.[17] Protect all the unborn children of our land, watch over them like a hen watches over her chicks.[18] Blessed is He that cometh in the name of the Lord.[19]

References: (1)Psalms 127:3-5; (2)Luke 16:15; (3)Isaiah 57:5,13,21; (4)Mark 10:15; (5)Mark 10:14; (6)Mark 10:16; (7)Acts 11:18; (8)Acts 5:29; (9)Acts 11:18; (10)2 Corinthians 5:21; (11)Daniel 9:3-5; (12)Psalms 33:22; (13)Philippians 2:10-11; (14)Proverbs 3:5; (15)James 4:8; (16)Deuteronomy 33:27; (17)Deuteronomy 33:29; (18)Matthew 23:37; (19)Matthew 23:39.

Addictions

Key Thought: When we are powerless over our addictions, we can avail ourselves of a Power greater than ourselves.

Key Scripture: *"Stand fast therefore in the liberty wherewith Christ hath made us free, and be not entangled again with the yoke of bondage" (Gal. 5:1).*

Prayer: Heavenly Father, I thank you for who you are and for all you can do for those who turn their hearts to you. Many in our society are addicted to various substances, behaviors, ideologies and people, but they are forgetting you. Bring healing to these addictive personalities who put other gods before you.[1] Remove their blindness; help them to see their idolatry and be set free.

Father, you sent Jesus to preach the gospel to the poor, heal the broken-hearted, preach deliverance to the captives and the recovering of sight to the blind. You have also promised to set at liberty those who are bruised.[2]

Lord, where there is sin in the addicts' lives, show it to them. Grant them hearts of godly sorrow and lead them to repentance.[3] Let them say, "Yes, Lord, that is sin, I need you," and receive your salvation and cleansing by your blood.[4]

Where there are unhealed hurts or wounds in their lives that are doorways for their addiction, show them to them and help them acknowledge them as true.[5] Then, Lord, bring your healing love to their hearts and heal each wound and hurt.[6]

Lord, show forth your grace to all those who are in bondage to various addictions — help them to escape, enlighten their eyes and revive them in the midst of their bondage.[7]

Be with _____

_____ who suffers from an addiction to

_____ .

Call him/her forth from his/her bondage into the glorious liberty that is reserved for your children.[8] Help him/her to fully realize that if you set someone free, they are truly free indeed.[9] Save them. Heal them. Deliver them.

There is no God like you, O Lord.[10] I praise your holy name. You will turn again and have compassion upon our people. You will subdue our iniquities and you will cast all our sins into the depths of the sea.[11]

Help all those who are set free through faith in your name to stand fast in the liberty wherewith you have set them free, so that they would not be entangled again with a yoke of bondage.[12] Strengthen them by your Spirit in their inner man.[13]

Thank you that you will never leave them nor forsake them[14] and whenever they are tempted to fall back into addictive habit patterns you will show them the way of escape.[15]

Thank you, Father, for setting them free and bringing them into the glorious liberty of the sons of God.[16]

References: *(1)Deuteronomy 5:7; (2)Luke 4:18; (3)2 Corinthians 7:10; (4)1 John 1:9; (5)John 8:32; (6)Psalms 147:3; (7)Ezra 9:8; (8)Romans 8:21; (9)John 8:36; (10)Micah 7:18; (11)Micah 7:19; (12)Galatians 5:1; (13)Ephesians 3:16; (14)Hebrews 13:5; (15)1 Corinthians 10:13; (16)Romans 8:21.*

The Aging

Key Thought: Elderly people have much to teach us about life.

Key Scripture: *"Blessed be the Lord, which hath not left thee this day without a kinsman, that his name may be famous in Israel. And he shall be unto thee a restorer of thy life, and a nourisher of thine old age" (Ruth 4:14-15).*

Prayer: Lord God, our Father and our Creator, I lift up to you the elderly people of our land — the able-bodied and mentally alert as well as those who need special care in nursing homes, Alzheimer's patients and all others. Be their Redeemer-kinsman, Lord, and restore their lives and nourish their old age.[1]

Bless the care-givers who watch out for the needs of our growing elderly population, Lord. Teach them to wait upon you for the strength they need. How I thank you, Father, that all those who wait upon you shall renew their strength. They shall mount up with wings as eagles; they shall run, and not be weary; and they shall walk, and not faint.[2]

At this moment, Father, I pray specifically for
_____ who is/are facing the challenges of aging. Bring many into their/his/her life(ves) who will be sensitive to their needs, having compassion on the elderly, loving them with empathy, courtesy and respect.[3] I pray, also, for all the family members of these (this) aging person/people. Help them not to be overcome with worry or anxiety about their

71

loved ones, but bless them with your special peace that passes all understanding as they care for their loved one(s).[4]

Come against all those who would discriminate against or even abuse the elderly, Lord. Move on the hearts of all of our people to show their elders honor, respect and love.[5]

As our citizens reach old age, Lord, I pray that you will enable them to be gracious, to honor you by walking in righteousness [6] and to be able to say with the Psalmist, "The steps of a good man are ordered by the Lord: and he delighteth in his way. Though he fall, he shall not be utterly cast down: for the Lord upholdeth him with his hand. I have been young, and now am old; yet have I not seen the righteous forsaken, nor his seed begging bread."[7] Thank you, Lord, for your faithfulness.

I pray that the aging will draw near to you, [8] so that they will be able to spend all eternity with you. May every aged person receive Jesus Christ as Lord and have eternal life.[9] Empower the elderly folks who know you to be a constant witness to your saving grace as they share with others who need to know you.[10]

Empower the aging people who know you to be able to say with Paul, "For all things are for your sakes, that the abundant grace might through the thanksgiving of many redound to the glory of God. For which cause we faint not; but though our outward man perish, yet the inward man is renewed day by day."[11]

Father, I ask that you strengthen them.[12] Supply all of their needs.[13] Prosper them financially.[14] Protect them and keep them safe.[15] Guide them in your wisdom [16] and quicken their mortal bodies by your Holy Spirit.[17]

Your promises, Lord, are so exciting and uplifting to people of all ages. Those who are planted in your house shall flourish. They shall bring forth fruit in old age. Thank you, Jesus, for the care you extend to your children of all ages. You are my Rock and there is no unrighteousness in you.[18]

Help the elderly people who know you to realize that no matter how old they are, they are of great use to you and your kingdom. The glory of the aged is the gray head.[19] Lead the elderly to teach the young your truth and to pray for your body, Lord.

Thank you, Father, for my parents, grandparents and other ancestors who worked so hard to provide for the future generations. Help me always to remember their sacrifices and may all their prayers be fulfilled in this generation and the generation to come.

References: (1)Ruth 4:15; (2)Isaiah 40:31; (3)1 Peter 3:8; (4)Philippians 4:7; (5)Leviticus 19:32; (6)1 Timothy 6:11; (7)Psalms 37:23-25; (8)James 4:8; (9)John 3:16; (10)Acts 1:8; (11)2 Corinthians 4:15-16; (12)Isaiah 40:31; (13)Philippians 4:19; (14)3 John 2; (15)Psalms 4:8; (16)Proverbs 2:6; (17)Romans 8:11; (18)Psalms 92:13-15; (19)Proverbs 20:29.

The American Family

Key Thought: Seldom is there a broken home when the family altar is kept up.

Key Scripture: *"See, I will send you the prophet Elijah before that great and dreadful day of the Lord comes. He will turn the hearts of the fathers to their children, and the hearts of the children to their fathers; or else I will come and strike the land with a curse"* (Mal. 4:5,6, NIV).

Prayer: Heavenly Father, you instituted the family to be the cornerstone of society. But all around I see so many families falling prey to the prevailing moods and philosophies of our day. You, Lord, have promised to come to all who call upon you in spirit and in truth.[1] The hour is coming, and now is, when the true worshippers shall worship you in Spirit and in truth, for I know, Father, that you seek such to worship you.[2] I pray for the families of our nation, that you would strengthen their commitment to you and to each other. Help families to pray together and to seek you together, Lord, so that our nation will become strong once again.

Through the power of your Spirit, Lord, I ask you to intervene in all families so that children will learn to obey their parents in you simply because this is right for them.[3] Help our young people never to forget the importance of the first commandment with a promise: to honor their fathers and mothers that it may be well with them and so they may live long on the earth.[4]

Lord, help fathers to understand their importance to their children and our nation, to take their rightful stand under your Lordship, to lead and to care for their families. Give them wisdom so that they would not provoke their children to wrath, but would bring them up in your nurture and admonition.[5]

Help us to learn how to submit to one another in reverent fear of you,[6] and to remember that the family represents the spiritual relationship between you, Lord Jesus, and your Church.[7] I pray for husbands throughout our country, that they would love their wives as you loved your Church and gave yourself for it.[8] I pray for wives, that they would reverence their husbands and submit to them as unto you, Lord.[9]

I pray for the members of my family:_____ _____. Watch over them, Lord.[10] Protect them.[11] Lead each one to always put you first.[12]

I thank you, Master, that I am a member of your body, of your flesh and of your bones. Help us never to forget that it was for this cause that a man should leave his father and mother in order to be joined to his wife, and they two should become one flesh. This is a great mystery, Lord, help us to understand that the relationships in our families speak to us of the most important relationship in life — our relationship with you.[13]

Guard our families, Lord, and keep them safe. Thank you for planting a hedge of protection around my family and the families of all who love you. Cultivate that hedge,

Father, around the homes of your people, and around all that we have. Bless the work of our hands, and increase our substance in the land.[14]

Deliver families from the enemy,[15] O my God, for he seeks to destroy our society by destroying families. [16] Defend your people from all who rise up against them.[17]

Deliver us from the workers of iniquity. We will sing of your power, Lord, and we will sing aloud of your mercy. For you are our defense and refuge in the day of trouble. Unto you, O my strength, will we sing: for you are our defense and you are the God of our mercy.[18]

References: (1)John 4:23; (2)John 4:24; (3)Ephesians 6:1; (4)Ephesians 6:2,3; (5)Ephesians 6:4; (6)Ephesians 5:21; (7)Ephesians 5:23; (8)Ephesians 5:25; (9)Ephesians 5:22; (10)Psalms 33:18; (11)Psalms 91:10; (12)Matthew 6:33; (13)Ephesians 5:32-33; (14)Job 1:10; (15)Matthew 6:13; (16)John 10:10; (17)Psalms 62:6; (18)Psalms 59:2,16,17.

The Armed Forces

Key Thought: Valiant men and women guard our nation — and all our freedoms — from watchposts around the world.

Key Scripture: *"He that dwelleth in the secret place of the most High shall abide under the shadow of the Almighty. I will say of the Lord, He is my refuge and my fortress: my God; in him will I trust. Surely he shall deliver thee from the snare of the fowler, and from the noisome pestilence. He shall cover thee with his feathers, and under his wings shalt thou trust: his truth shall be thy shield and buckler"* *(Ps. 91:1-4).*

Prayer: Lord Jesus, you prophesied correctly that there would always be wars and rumors of wars.[1] Because this is true, we need our armed forces to defend us from those nations that plot against us.

Bless our Commander-in-Chief, the President of the United States. Give him wisdom, Father, as he makes the decisions that affect the defense of our nation. Be with him, the Secretary of State, the Secretary of Defense, the Chairman of the Joint Chiefs of Staff, the chiefs of each military force, the generals, admirals and other officers of our armed forces. Bless especially the men and women of the army, navy, air force, marines, coast guard, and other services as they work hard to protect us in lonely places around the world.

Thank you for the veterans of the armed forces who have sacrificed so much to protect our land and our freedom. Many thousands have died in the service of our country and we thank you, Father, for giving them the courage and honor to lay down their lives for us. We acknowledge the truth that no man or woman has greater love than that which is demonstrated by their willingness to lay down their lives for another.[2]

Help the members of our armed forces to realize that by serving our country they are serving you. Help each one to see that he or she is your minister for good, that they do not bear the sword in vain because it is their divine commission to execute wrath upon those who do evil.[3]

Surround our servicepeople with your love, O Lord. Anoint the military chaplains to preach your Word with clarity and conviction so that many military personnel will come to know you in a personal way.

I pray especially for _____ _____ who serve(s) you and this nation in the armed forces. Be a very present help to him/her.[4] Help him/her to realize that you are with him/her always,[5] and to remember that you will never leave nor forsake him/her.[6] Keep him/her from evil at all times.[7] Protect him/her and give him/her a love for your Word and for Christian fellowship. Remind him/her of your promise that if he/she will abide under your shadow, that even if a thousand fall at his/her side and if ten thousand fall at his/her right hand, it will not come near him/her.[8]

Thank you for all the Christian people who minister to our servicepeople around the world. Bless them in their important ministries. Fill the Christian servicemen's centers with your Spirit so that earnest seekers will come and be won to you.

Lord, I beseech you in behalf of our nation and the armed forces who protect us, that when war clouds threaten on the horizon, you will lead our people to prayer. Then shall you go forth, Lord, and you will fight against those nations that become our enemies in the same way you often fought in behalf of your people in the Old Testament.[9]

Fight for us, Lord, in the same way that you fought against the Egyptians[10] when Israel was oppressed by them. You are our strength and our song and you have become our salvation. You always triumph gloriously, and you throw the horse and his rider into the sea. You, O Lord, are a man of war. Your right hand has become glorious in power, and your right hand dashes our enemies in pieces. In the greatness of your excellency you overthrow those who rise up against you and your people. With the blast of your nostrils you can dry up a flood. When our enemies pursue us, you will overtake them. Who is like you, O Lord? You are glorious in holiness, fearful in praises and you always do wonders.[11]

Guide our armed forces, Lord, to do mighty exploits in your wonderful name.[12]

References: (1)Mark 13:7; (2)John 15:13; (3)Romans 13:4; (4)Psalms 46:1; (5)Matthew 28:20; (6)Hebrews 13:5; (7)Luke 11:4; (8)Psalms 91:1,7; (9)Zechariah 14:3; (10)Exodus 14:14; (11)Exodus 15:1-11; (12)Daniel 11:28.

Children

Key Thought: Jesus loves the children of the world.

Key Scripture: *"Train up a child in the way he should go: and when he is old, he will not depart from it"* (Prov. 22:6).

Prayer: Thank you, Father, for the innocence and trust that children possess. Lord, remind the parents of America of their responsibility to care for and nurture their children, to bring them up in your nurture and admonition,[1] to never provoke them to wrath,[2] to show the children what you are like through parental example.

You have pointed out that whoever receives a little child in your name is actually receiving you. Thank you, Lord Jesus, for your love of children and for all the wonderful promises of your Word.[3]

When you called a little child to come to you, you pointed out the truth that we need to be converted, to become as little children, in order to enter the kingdom of heaven.[4] You then went on to warn us to take heed not to despise any of your little ones, because in heaven their angels are always beholding your face.[5] Thank you for giving your angels charge over our children, Lord, to guard and protect them.[6] Release your angels to do battle on behalf of the children of America.

Protect our children, Lord, from all experiences and individuals that would violate them. In an age when we hear so much about abuse — physical, sexual, emotional, ritual — I intercede in behalf of the children of America, and I ask you, Lord, to intervene in the lives of these little ones, keep them safe and stay the hands of those who would seek to inflict damage upon them.[7]

Those who seek you, Lord, shall not want any good thing. Call the children of America unto you, and lead them to salvation through the word of the Gospel and faith in Jesus Christ as their Lord and Savior.[8]

Give our children the hearts of true disciples, may they be taught of the Lord and have great peace.[9] Fill them with your Spirit.[10] Pour your Spirit upon them that they may live holy and righteous lives before you as your servants and handmaidens.[11] Give them your enduring hope as the anchor of their souls.[12]

I pray that the children of our nation will be filled with your wisdom, understanding and knowledge.[13] That they will acknowledge you in all their ways and you will direct their paths.[14]

How excellent is your lovingkindness, O God! Therefore, the children of our land are able to put their trust under the shadow of your wings. You have promised that they shall be satisfied with the fatness of your house and you shall make them drink from the river of your pleasures. For with you is the fountain of life. In your light we shall see light.[15]

Help America to show your truth and your ways to its children. To teach your little ones to love you. To show to the younger generation your praises, your strength and the wonderful works you have done so that they would set their hope in you, remember your works and keep your commandments.[16]

I praise you, O Lord, for you have strengthened the bars of your gates, and you have blessed the children under our care.[17] Let every thing that has breath praise you, Lord, including the children of our land.[18] Bless the children, Lord, and watch over them.

References: (1)Ephesians 6:4; (2)Colossians 3:21; (3)Matthew 18:5-6; (4)Matthew 18:2-3; (5)Matthew 18:10; (6)Matthew 4:6; (7)Isaiah 49:25; (8)Mark 16:15-16; (9)Isaiah 54:13; (10)Ephesians 5:18; (11)Acts 2:17,39; (12)Hebrews 6:19; (13)Proverbs 2:6; (14)Proverbs 3:6; (15)Psalms 36:7-9; (16)Psalms 78:1-7; (17)Psalms 147:12-13; (18)Psalms 150:6.

The Church

Key Thought: The world at its worst calls for the Church at its best.

Key Scripture: *"Upon this rock I will build my church: and the gates of hell shall not prevail against it. And I will give unto thee the keys of the kingdom of heaven: and whatsoever thou shalt bind on earth shall be bound in heaven: and whatsoever thou shalt loose on earth shall be loosed in heaven" (Matt. 16:18,19).*

Prayer: Heavenly Father, I thank you for adopting me into your worldwide family. For as many as are led by your Spirit are your sons. I thank you that I have not received the spirit of bondage again to fear; but because of your great love for me, I have received the Spirit of adoption that enables me to cry, "Abba, Father."[1]

Thank you for building your Church, O God. During this age of intensifying spiritual warfare, I pray that the Church will enter into your promise that the gates of hell will never be able to prevail against it.[2] I ask that the influence of the powers of darkness against the Church in America be broken and destroyed. Strengthen your Church in America and around the world so that we will effectively go and teach all nations, baptizing them in the name of the Father, and of the Son, and of the Holy Ghost. Through your Spirit we are enabled to teach people to observe your commandments. Thank you for being with us unto the end of the world.[3]

Grant a spirit of wisdom, revelation and knowledge to the pastors, church leaders and all Christians throughout our country. May we walk in the full knowledge of who you are, Lord Jesus, and all that you are able to do.[4] Through your Holy Spirit working in and through us, the eyes of our understanding will be enlightened, we will know the hope of your calling and the riches of the glory of your inheritance in the saints.[5] Help our spiritual leaders to realize the truth that unless you are building the house, those who build it labor in vain.[6]

May the unity of your body increase, Lord Jesus, as we face the difficult and trying circumstances of these last days. Grant us grace to fulfill your prayer that all of us would be one as you and the Father are one. May your people become one in you so that the world may believe that the Father sent you. Jesus, dwell in our midst as the Father dwells in you that the Church may be made perfect in unity.[7]

I ask that your Word would dwell richly within me and my brothers and sisters in all wisdom. In this way we will be able to teach and admonish one another in psalms and hymns and spiritual songs, singing with grace in our hearts unto you.[8] Help us to encourage, inspire and edify your people.

Give great boldness unto me and all your servants as we face the issues of our day.[9] Help us to fight the good fight of faith in your power and might, to lay hold on eternal life whereunto we have been called.[10] Through your grace and power we shall be able to remain steadfast, unmoveable, always abounding in your work, for I know that our labors will never be in vain in you.[11] Help all of your people to remain steady in the important work you have called your body to accomplish.

Let a spirit of prayer fill your Church and bring a renewed devotion to prayer and intercession.[12] I pray that your Church will lay hold of the truth that the effectual, fervent prayer of the righteous is powerful and avails much.[13]

O Lord, revive your work in the midst of the years. Make your will known to the Church.[14] Send revival to your people till the glory of the Lord shall cover America and all the earth as the waters cover the sea.[15]

References: *(1)Romans 8:14-15; (2)Matthew 16:18-19; (3)Matthew 28:19-20; (4)Ephesians 1:17; (5)Ephesians 1:18; (6)Psalms 127:1; (7)John 17:21,23; (8)Colossians 3:16; (9)1 Timothy 3:13; (10)1 Timothy 6:12; (11)1 Corinthians 15:58; (12)Colossians 4:2; (13)James 5:16; (14)Habakkuk 3:2; (15)Habakkuk 2:14.*

The Clergy

Key Thought: Our pastors and ministers need us to back them up with daily prayer.

Key Scripture: *"Turn, O backsliding children, saith the Lord; for I am married unto you: and I will take you one of a city, and two of a family, and I will bring you to Zion: And I will give you pastors according to mine heart, which shall feed you with knowledge and understanding" (Jer. 3:14-15).*

Prayer: Thank you for all the gifts you have imparted unto your people, Lord Jesus. Thank you for the apostles, prophets, evangelists, pastors and teachers and other leaders you have set into the body for the perfecting of your saints, for the work of the ministry, for the edifying of your body. Through them, Lord, you will lead us into the unity of the faith and in knowledge of you. Help your people to pray for their pastors and leaders daily so that we can attain to your goal of becoming a perfect body, unto the measure of the stature of your fullness. Henceforth, dear Lord, I ask that your ministers and prophets would establish us so firmly in your Word that we would never again be tossed to and fro or carried about with every wind of doctrine, by the sleight of man and cunning craftiness. Help us to be mature enough that we will always speak the truth in love so that we may grow up into you in all things.[1]

Bless our pastors, Lord. Give your people the grace to understand them and to encourage them, and help the special people you have called into ministry to be like David who encouraged himself in you.[2] When David was greatly distressed, as so many ministers are today because of the pressures and disappointments they face daily, he turned to prayer. Help your people to pray for all who have spiritual authority over them, and help our leaders to take hold of you through daily prayer, to rejoice evermore, to pray without ceasing and to give thanks in everything, for this is your will.[3]

Thank you for preparing your throne in the heavens, O Lord. Your kingdom rules over all. I bless you and I praise you for the ministers of your Word who take the prophet's stance in behalf of you in our nation today. Bless them, their spouses, their families and associates. Protect them. May they ever bless you as they do your pleasure, Lord.[4]

I pray especially for my pastor, _____ _____. Guide him/her, Father, and give him/her wisdom as he/she does your work. Lead him/her to always take heed to the sacred ministry you have given to him/her, and remind him/her that he/she received it from you so that he/she will be able to fulfill it.[5] May he/she never grow weary in well-doing even when so many fail to express appreciation for his/her labors.[6] I ask you to strengthen his/her wife/husband, _____ , and their children, _____ . Help me to be their friend.

May the leaders of our land turn to the men and women of God for prayer support and biblical guidance as they face the decisions of our day. Anoint the clergy, Lord, and remind them that their sufficiency is of you,[7] your strength is made perfect in weakness,[8] and you have made them able ministers of your New Testament.[9] Help our pastors and leaders to abide in you, Lord Jesus, for without you we can do nothing,[10] but through you we can accomplish all things.[11]

Continue to impart wisdom through your Spirit and your Word to the ministers of your Church, Lord Jesus. I thank you that you are building your Church, and the gates of hell will not prevail against it.[12] In view of this truth, Lord, I ask you to fill our pastors and leaders with your Spirit so that they will be able to produce the fruit of your Spirit in all the relationships and responsibilities of their lives — love, peace, joy, patience, meekness, gentleness, faithfulness, goodness and self-control.[13]

Help your ministers to take a prophetic stance before your people and the world. To speak forth your Word with boldness, and to tell your plan. To pray for your people and to gently lead them into all truth.[14] Thank you for giving the keys of your kingdom to your men and women who minister before you. Whatsoever they bind on earth will be bound in heaven, and whatsoever they loose on earth will be loosed in heaven.[15] Praise your holy name!

Thank you for your warning, Lord, that the fear of man always brings a snare.[16] Deliver your pastors, ministers and leaders from the fear of man and, indeed, from all fear, for fear brings torment and it is not your will for us.[17]

I praise you, Lord, and I ask you to reveal your truth to the clergy of our land. Help them to trust your promise that all who fear you and delight in your commandments will see your blessing in the lives of his/her progeny. The generation of the upright will be blessed, and wealth and riches shall be in their houses, because your righteousness, O Lord, endures forever.[18]

References: (1)Ephesians 4:11-15; (2)1 Samuel 30:6; (3)1 Thessalonians 5:16-18; (4)Psalms 103:19-22; (5)Colossians 4:17; (6)2 Thessalonians 3:13; (7)2 Corinthians 3:5; (8)2 Corinthians 12:9; (9)2 Corinthians 3:6; (10)John 15:4-5; (11)Philippians 4:13; (12)Matthew 16:18; (13)Galatians 5:22-23; (14)Acts 4:31; (15)Matthew 16:19; (16)Proverbs 29:25; (17)1 John 4:18; (18)Psalms 112:1-3.

Compassion and Love

Key Thought: A loving word can heal and bless.

Key Scripture: *"Inasmuch as ye have done it unto one of the least of these my brethren, ye have done it unto me"* *(Matt. 25:40).*

Prayer: Dear God, our heavenly Father, I thank you that you loved the world so much that you gave your only begotten Son that whosoever would believe in Him would have everlasting life.[1] Lead many in America today to receive your free gift of love for as many as receive your Son also receive the power to become your sons, through belief in your name.[2] Send revival to America, Lord, so that men, women and young people would respond to your call to love you with all their hearts, minds and strength and to love their neighbors as themselves.[3] Cover our nation with your love, Father, and may our citizens see your love reflected in the Church of Jesus Christ, your Son. For by our love will all men know that we are your children.[4]

Forgive our nation of its hard-heartedness, Lord. Help all of us to remember that we must never shut our hands from the poor.[5] Lead our citizens to become generous with all that you have given to us by opening their hands wide unto all those who are poor and needy in our land.[6] Help me and all believers to remember that we were once like bondmen in the land of Egypt, but you, Lord, redeemed us and brought us into the Promised Land of your Kingdom.[7] Even as I reflect upon this wonderful truth my heart is filled with love for I realize I am greatly blessed by you for you had compassion on me.[8] Have compassion on the United States of America, Lord; reveal your never-failing love to our people.

Lord, you are merciful and gracious, slow to anger and plenteous in mercy.[9] Fill us with your Spirit so that we may reflect those same attributes as a nation under you. Let your tender mercies come to our nation that we may live.[10] Thank you for being so gracious to our nation. You are full of compassion and of great mercy.[11]

Relieve the oppressed, judge the fatherless in your mercy and plead for the widow, Lord.[12] Help your Church to adhere to these same values.

Though the Law was given by Moses, grace and truth came to us through you, Lord Jesus.[13] Now abide faith, hope and love but the greatest of these is love.[14] Thank you for showing us the more excellent way of love.[15]

Father, shed your love abroad in our hearts by your Holy Spirit so that we may be able to join you in showing people everywhere the more excellent way of your love.[16]

Teach the people of our nation to follow your love commandment, Lord, for you said that you gave us a new commandment, that we should love one another.[17] Remind our citizens of the high value you place on adherence to the Golden Rule, and lead all of us to understand that if a person loves another person he has fulfilled your law[18] for love never works ill toward our neighbors.[19] I thank you that all the Law is fulfilled through love.[20]

Revive our land, Lord, so that our citizens will respond to your love. Teach husbands and wives to love each other,[21] let the Church demonstrate your love to the world,[22] and help all of us to love in deed and in truth, not only in word.[23] Help me to seize every opportunity you give me to love my fellow-citizens.

Lord God, I thank you that you are love.[24] Help us to remember that because you so loved us, we ought also to love one another.[25] Bring the supremacy of love to our nation once more, Father. May each individual arise out of his or her fear and begin to walk in love for your perfect love casts out all fear.[26] Let your love cover our land as the waters cover the sea. Thank you for sharing your love so freely with us.

References: (1)John 3:16; (2)John 1:12; (3)Matthew 22:37-39; (4)John 13:35; (5)Deuteronomy 15:7; (6)Deuteronomy 15:8; (7)Deuteronomy 15:15; (8)1 Samuel 23:21; (9)Psalms 103:8; (10)Psalms 119:77; (11)Psalms 145:8; (12)Isaiah 1:17; (13)John 1:17; (14)1 Corinthians 13:13; (15)1 Corinthians 12:31; (16)Romans 5:5; (17)John 13:34; (18)Romans 13:8; (19)Romans 13:10; (20)Galatians 5:14; (21)Ephesians 5:25-29; (22)1 John 3:11; (23)1 John 3:18; (24)1 John 4:8; (25)1 John 4:11; (26)1 John 4:18.

The Congress of the United States

Key Thought: "Whatever makes men good Christians makes them good citizens" (Daniel Webster).

Key Scripture: *"The Spirit of the Lord spake by me, and his word was in my tongue. The God of Israel said, the Rock of Israel spoke to me. He that ruleth over men must be just, ruling in the fear of God"* (2 Sam. 23:2-3).

Prayer: Lord God, Father of our Lord and Savior Jesus Christ, have mercy upon our country. Guide our leaders to know you, to seek your wisdom and to receive salvation through faith in Jesus Christ. I pray for the senators and representatives who serve us in the U.S. Capitol. I ask your blessing on each senator and representative and their families. Keep them from evil, Lord, and help them always to see clearly.[1]

I pray especially for the senators from my state: _____ , and also for the congressperson who represents my legislative district: _____ _____ . May they always rule in fear of you, Lord, and help them always to strive to be just and fair in their dealings with their constituents, their fellow congresspeople and the other branches of our government.

God, grant that the members of the U.S. Congress will become as the light of the morning, when the sun rises, even a morning without clouds — as the tender grass springing out of the earth by clear shining after rain.[2]

May all the members of the U.S. Congress — both senators and representatives — follow after truth at all times. Remind each one, Father, that if a ruler hearkens unto lies, all his servants become wicked.[3] The fear of man always brings a snare, Lord, but everyone who puts his trust in you will be safe. Reveal this to the members of the U.S. Congress, and show them that while many will always seek their favor, every man's judgment comes from you. Teach them that an unjust man is an abomination to the just, and he that is upright in his way is an abomination to the wicked.[4] Thank you, Lord, for the practical wisdom presented in your Word. Let your Word be exalted by these leaders.

Help me, and all your people, to submit ourselves to every ordinance of man for your sake, Lord, for I know this is your will for your people, and in so doing we will be able to put to silence the foolishness of ignorant men.[5]

Thank you for the freedom we enjoy as citizens of the United States of America. Help me never to use my freedom as a cloak of maliciousness, but only as your servant, Lord. Help me and my fellow believers always to honor you, love the brotherhood, fear you and honor all those who have authority over us.[6]

Restore godly humility to our land, Lord, so that the leaders and people of our nation will remember that the kingdom is yours, and that you are the governor among the nations.[7] Thank you for the righteous example of Joseph, the young man you delivered out of all his afflictions. It was you, O Lord, who gave him favor and wisdom in the sight of Pharaoh, and you made Joseph governor over Egypt and all the house of the king.[8] Help our congresspeople remember that you are the one who appoints our leaders and that there is no power but of you, O God, and the powers that be are ordained by you.[9]

In your name, Lord God, I come against all the division and partisanship that creates confusion and stymies progress in the work of the government of our land. I know that you are not the author of confusion, but you are the originator of peace.[10] A truly wise person, Lord, you have pointed out, should live a godly life with the meekness that comes from wisdom. Where there is bitter envying and strife, as we sometimes see in the halls of Congress, we know that the enemy of our souls is doing his work. Such a mind-set that leads to this behavior does not descend from above because it is earthly, sensual and devilish. Lord, I ask that you would sow the fruit of righteousness, without hypocrisy, in the hearts and lives of the members of the U.S. Congress.[11]

Thank you for our representatives in government, Father. Help them not only to represent us but also to represent you.

References: (1)*Luke 11:4;* (2)*2 Samuel 23:2-4;* (3)*Proverbs 28:12;* (4)*Proverbs 29:25-27;* (5)*1 Peter 2:13-15;* (6)*1 Peter 2:16-17;* (7)*Psalms 22:28;* (8)*Acts 7:9-10;* (9)*Romans 13:1;* (10)*1 Corinthians 14:33;* (11)*James 3:14-18.*

The Cultural War

Key Thought: Ninety-four percent of Americans believe in God.

Key Scripture: *"The fool hath said in his heart, There is no God. They are corrupt, they have done abominable works, there is none that doeth good. The Lord looked down from heaven upon the children of men, to see if there were any that did understand, and seek God"* (Ps. 14:1,2).

Prayer: Heavenly Father, the very foundations of our nation are being assaulted in this hour by the forces of wickedness, secular humanism and moral relativism. Many are losing sight of the Judeo-Christian ethic, with its moral absolutes, upon which our nation was founded. Strengthen our resolve to hold the line, to be true to you and to not be led astray.

Lord, I ask you to open up the old paths that have become overgrown by ungodly philosophies. Reveal the good way to our people so that they might walk therein and find rest for their souls.[1] Remove not the ancient landmark that was set by our fathers.[2] Do not permit the pagans of this modern day to remove the old landmark, O mighty Redeemer. I plead before you, Father, the cause of our nation that is in danger of losing its moral bearings.[3]

In the cultural war that divides America today, I ask, O Lord, that you would be our Victor, that your Word would once again be held in the high esteem that our fathers felt. Call all our people unto yourself, Lord, and be jealous for them so that they will be born again, not of corruptible seed, but of incorruptible, by your Word which lives and abides forever. [4]

Restore to our nation a desire to return to the traditional values that made us a strong people. As our fathers did, so may we do forevermore. [5] May our churches, clergy, media, schools, families and other institutions give high regard to prayer and your Word once more as we did in former years.

Father, your Word says that we do not wrestle against flesh and blood, but against the powers of darkness. [6] Destroy the evil agendas that the enemy has sown in the minds of our people. [7] Be mighty in America, Lord, and pull down reasonings and every high thing that exalts itself against the knowledge of God. Let every thought of our people be brought into obedience to Christ. [8] With you, O God, all things are possible. [9]

Stem the tide of opinion that rejects your commandments in favor of keeping the traditions of men. [10] Thank you for your commandments, Father. Remind our nation of the need to honor our fathers and mothers, and all the other statutes you have given to us. Reach into the hearts of our people, Father. Convict them of their sins and convince them of their need for salvation through Jesus Christ the Lord.

Thank you for the heritage of our nation, Lord. You are the God of our fathers, [11] and you are my God. You made a covenant with our forefathers and this wonderful covenant is with us, even us, who are alive this day. [12] Let a double portion of your Spirit be upon this present generation of Christians in America today.[13] Thank you for the good heritage we have as citizens of the United States.[14]

Because the roots of our nation are holy, it is possible for us, the branches of the tree, to be holy too.[15] Bring your holiness to our nation, Lord.

In your mighty name, Lord Jesus Christ, I come against the powerful forces that endeavor to undermine traditional values in our society today. Restore unto us the excellence of dignity and character.[16] Thank you for setting the land before us. Through the power of your Holy Spirit, help your people to go in and possess the land which you gave unto our forefathers.[17] You, Lord, are the portion of our inheritance.[18] Praise your name!

References: (1)Jeremiah 6:16; (2)Proverbs 22:28; (3)Proverbs 23:10-11; (4)1 Peter 1:23; (5)2 Kings 17:41; (6)Ephesians 6:12; (7)John 3:19; (8)2 Corinthians 10:5; (9)Matthew 19:26; (10)Mark 7:9; (11)Exodus 3:6; (12)Deuteronomy 5:3; (13)2 Kings 2:9; (14)Psalms 16:6; (15)Romans 11:16; (16)Genesis 49:3; (17)Deuteronomy 1:8; (18)Psalms 16:5.

Deception

Key Thought: "The fact is that truth is your best friend, no matter what the circumstances are" (Abraham Lincoln).

Key Scripture: *"And Jesus answered and said unto them, Take heed that no man deceive you. For many shall come in my name, saying, I am Christ; and shall deceive many. And ye shall hear of wars and rumours of wars: see that ye be not troubled: for all these things must come to pass, but the end is not yet" (Matt. 24:4-6).*

Prayer: Help us, heavenly Father, to walk in the truth so that we will not fall prey to deception in any form. Protect our nation from ungodly philosophies that threaten to deceive so many and have already blinded the minds of some.

I come against Satan in your mighty name, Lord Jesus, because I know he seeks to deceive our people and to destroy our land. By his sorceries all the nations of the world will one day be deceived.[1] Protect America from Satan's lies, Lord God, I pray. Cursed be the deceiver.[2]

Do away with the workers of iniquity in our land, Father. Deal with all those who speak peace to their neighbors but carry mischief in their hearts.[3] Open the eyes of all those who say, "Peace, peace" when there is no peace.[4]

Plant your hedge of protection around the United States of America, Father, so that our leaders and people would not become the victims of deception in any form.[5] Thank you for warning us about the false Christs and false prophets who will endeavor to seduce your people through signs and wonders.[6] Help your Church to ever be watchful and discerning so that we would always be able to recognize deception when it appears.

Grant the gift of discernment to believers so that they would never be deceived.[7] Protect our young people and adults from spiritual deception, Lord.

Empower your Church to take the offensive against the enemy's lying schemes by exposing his works of darkness whenever they are revealed.[8] Keep your people from ever participating in the enemy's beguiling lures. Keep us from evil, Lord.[9]

Many false prophets, occultists, astrologers, spiritists and other diviners are leading many within our nation astray, Lord. Put a stop to their offenses and lead those who participate in the unfruitful works of darkness into your marvelous kingdom of light.[10] Help me and all my fellow-believers to speak the truth in love so that many would be delivered and set free.[11] May none of us ever be guilty of saying that you have said something when you have in fact not spoken.[12] For us to do so is to take part in deception, a work of darkness.

Help me to take heed at all times so that I would never be deceived for many shall come in your name, Lord, and they will say that they are you and many will be deceived.[13] Give me the ability to recognize these false Christs when they appear.

Help me and my fellow-believers never to deceive ourselves.[14] Reveal to our nation that the wisdom of this world is foolishness with you, dear Father.[15]

Show to our people that the opposite of deception is truth, that the truth will set them free,[16] and that walking in the light of truth is far better than walking in the darkness of deception. Reveal to the victims of deception that they have been bewitched by Satan into not obeying the truth.[17] Let no man deceive my fellow-citizens through vain words.[18] Help Americans to beware lest anyone would spoil them through philosophy and vain deceit.[19]

Dear God, deal swiftly with all those who call evil good and good evil. Convict those who put darkness for light and light for darkness. Rebuke all those who put bitter for sweet and sweet for bitter.[20]

Through the power of your name and under the covering of your blood, I pray for _____ _____ who is/are the victim(s) of deception. Set him/her/them free, Father. Deliver him/her/them from evil.

References: (1)Revelation 18:23; (2)Malachi 1:14; (3)Psalms 28:3; (4)Jeremiah 6:14; (5)Job 1:10; (6)Mark 13:22; (7)1 Corinthians 12:10; (8)Ephesians 5:11; (9)Matthew 6:13; (10)1 Peter 2:9; (11)Ephesians 4:15; (12)Ezekiel 13:7; (13)Mark 13:5-6; (14)1 Corinthians 3:18; (15)1 Corinthians 3:19; (16)John 8:32; (17)Galatians 3:1; (18)Ephesians 5:6; (19)Colossians 2:8; (20)Isaiah 5:20.

Drug Abuse

Key Thought: There is a Power that is greater than ourselves.

Key Scripture: *"Ask, and it shall be given you; seek, and ye shall find; knock, and it shall be opened unto you: For every one that asketh receiveth; and he that seeketh findeth; and to him that knocketh it shall be opened"* (Matt. 7:7-8).

Prayer: Lord God, I come before your presence and I pray for all those who are deceived by the wickedness of substance abuse in the form of narcotics, alcohol, drugs and tobacco. Help each one to see the harm he/she is bringing to himself/herself and to others. As the fire devours the stubble and the flame consumes the chaff, those who practice drug abuse will find their roots becoming rotten and their blossoms disintegrating because they have cast away your law, O Lord, and they have despised your Word.[1]

You have told us not to be drunk with wine wherein is excess. Instead, you have commanded us to be filled with your Spirit, O Lord.[2] Fill me with your Spirit, Lord, so that I might bear the fruit of your Spirit (love, peace, joy, patience, meekness, gentleness, faithfulness, goodness and self-control) in all the relationships and responsibilities of my life.[3] May all addicts eventually enjoy that blessing as well.

Lord, you do not wish that any should perish, but that all should come to repentence.[4]Therefore, I pray that you would send anointed workers of your harvest to all addicts in our land to tell them the truth of the gospel that they would be saved.[5]

I pray that your Spirit would accompany the addicts of our country with restlessness until they find their complete and eternal rest in you, O Lord. Convict them of their sin and set them free from their addictions.

Father, you sent Jesus to destroy the works of the devil.[6] I ask you, in Jesus' name,[7] to rise up strong in your love and your power and destroy the works of the enemy in the lives of the drug addicts of America. Let them know the joy of your salvation.[8]

I pray especially for _____
_____ who is/are bound by his/her/their addiction(s). Set him/her/them free. Praise your mighty name!

Warn those who practice all the evil associated with drug addiction — the suppliers, sellers, pimps, prostitutes, users — and all others involved, that you are prepared to punish the evildoers.[9] Draw them unto yourself so that you can wash them clean through the blood of Jesus Christ.[10] Lead them to cease from their evil works, to learn to do well. Let them overcome the enemy through the blood of the Lamb and the word of their testimony.[11]

Bless all those who work with drug abusers — counselors, nurses, doctors, social workers, clergy, family members — lead them to put you first[12] and to pray for those under their care.[13] Give them words of wisdom[14] that will set the captives free.[15]

Lord, be very close to all those who have renounced their addictions. Enable them to stand fast in the liberty wherewith you have set them free so that they will never again become entangled with a yoke of bondage.[16]

References: *(1)Isaiah 5:24; (2)Ephesians 5:18; (3)Galatians 5:22-23; (4)2 Peter 3:9; (5)Matthew 9:38; (6)1 John 3:8; (7)John 16:23; (8)Psalms 51:12; (9)Jeremiah 13:21; (10)1 John 1:7; (11)Revelation 12:11; (12)Matthew 6:33; (13)James 5:16; (14)Proverbs 4:7; (15)Luke 4:18; (16)Galatians 5:1.*

The Economy

Key Thought: God has a plan.

Key Scripture: *"Except the Lord build the house, they labor in vain that build it"* (Ps. 127:1).

Prayer: Heavenly Father, I praise you and I thank you that you are plenteous in mercy[1] and your eyes are upon the righteous.[2] You are always ready to show yourself strong on their behalf.[3]

You, Lord, are able to do abundantly over and above all that we can ask or even think.[4] With men many things are impossible but with you all things are possible.[5]

Thank you that you have given me the gift of righteousness through faith in Jesus Christ,[6] and that the effectual, fervent prayer of the righteous person avails much and is of great effect.[7]

Father, our nation has handled her money sinfully through both foolish spending and financing ungodly programs. We have sinned. Please forgive us[8] and have mercy upon us.[9]

Even the heart of the king is in your hand, Lord, and you turn it whatever way you wish.[10] I pray that the hearts of our leaders and all our citizens would be in your hand today, and that in your great mercy you would turn them to righteousness through faith in Jesus Christ the Lord.[11]

Pour forth your Word in America, O God. Let it bring great change in our land. Let it be like fire and like the hammer that breaks the rock into pieces.[12]

Father God, loose revival in America.[13] Give us a harvest of souls for your kingdom.[14] Let that harvest be of such magnitude that the overwhelming majority of the people of our nation turn their hearts to you.[15]

Father, I pray on behalf of all our citizens, both the righteous and the unjust — have mercy, show forth your great love and kindness and bless our nation with financial prosperity and a sound economy.[16]

Be strong on behalf of your children in America,[17] and grant them economic prosperity, for you give the power to obtain wealth that you may establish and make plain your covenant with your people.[18]

You tell us in your Word that it is through wisdom that a house is built and by understanding it is established, and that by knowledge the chambers shall be filled with all precious and pleasant riches.[19]

All this wisdom, understanding and knowledge come from you, from your mouth, to those who seek it from you.[20]

Father, I pray that our president would turn to you for the wisdom, understanding and knowledge he needs, for you will not cast out those who come to you.[21]

I thank you for our president, Lord.[22] Work in him to will and to do your good pleasure.[23] Give him the wisdom, courage and character to make the right decisions on behalf of America, even when those decisions vary from what is considered politically correct for successful election campaigns.[24]

Likewise, raise up members of congress who will have the wisdom, courage and character to make the right decisions even when it does not seem politically expedient to do so. Remove those who refuse these things.[25]

Grant us the inner strength and the will to live within our means and to eliminate both deficit spending and excessive debt.[26]

I pray for the finances of our country to be administered wisely and fairly, for our taxes to be as low as possible and for wasteful and foolish spending to be stopped. Give the leaders in government, labor and business the will and the wisdom to work together and develop and implement the plans and strategies that will strengthen all areas of our economy.[27]

Bless the people of our land with skill, wisdom,[28] and jobs that pay well and are stable.[29]

Prosper the businesses of America with good profits so they can pay their employees well and have plenty of money left over to finance business growth.[30]

Deliver us from the schemes and devices of the evil one.[31]

Your Word says that those who give to the poor lend to you and that you will repay them. Lord, America has given much to the poor, both in our nation and around the world. Help us always to show compassion for the poor. Be merciful and repay us according to this promise.[32]

Pour your blessing on our land, and give us a sense of your vision and purpose for America. For blessed is the nation whose God is the Lord.[33]

References: *(1)Psalms 86:15; (2)Psalms 34:15; (3)2 Chronicles 16:9; (4)Ephesians 3:20; (5)Matthew 19:26; (6)Romans 5:17; (7)James 5:16; (8)Psalms 103:3; (9)Psalms 123:3; (10)Proverbs 21:1; (11)Philippians 3:9; (12)Jeremiah 23:29; (13)Habakkuk 3:2; (14)Matthew 9:37-38; (15)Lamentations 5:21; (16)Matthew 5:44-45; (17)Psalms 31:2; (18)Deuteronomy 8:18; (19)Proverbs 24:3-4; (20)Proverbs 2:6; (21)John 6:37; (22)1 Timothy 2:1-2; (23)Philippians 2:13; (24)Proverbs 2:6-9; (25)Psalms 75:6-7; (26)Ephesians 3:16; (27)Proverbs 8:14-16; (28)Daniel 1:17; (29)Philippians 4:19; (30)3 John 2; (31)Luke 11:4; (32)Proverbs 19:17; (33)Psalms 33:12.*

Education

Key Thought: Christianity is the mother of modern education.

Key Scripture: *"The fear of the Lord is the beginning of wisdom: a good understanding have all they that do his commandments: his praise endureth forever"* (Ps. 111:10).

Prayer: Lord, I thank you that I live in the United States of America where public education is provided for all children, where private and religious schools are free to impart their values to students and where colleges and universities prepare young people for lives of service. Bless the administrators, educators and other professionals who dedicate themselves to the important work of education. Guide school boards and commissioners of education with your wisdom. Help each one to know and apply the truth of your Word and to realize that the tongue of the wise uses knowledge rightly, but the mouth of fools pours out foolishness.[1]

Heavenly Father, inspire today's educators with a desire to follow you, to always seek to follow after that which is good,[2] so that they will always remember to be positive role models for our children and youths.

I ask you to remove evil from the schools of our land, preserve the students from all evil and preserve their souls.[3] Impart wisdom to our leaders so that they will know how to deal with violence, drug abuse, sexual immorality, and other evils that are coming against young people today.

Father, I ask that you will restore prayer and Bible reading to our public schools. May our teachers and students be reminded of their need to study to show themselves approved unto you, workmen who never need to be ashamed because they are rightly dividing your Word of truth.[4]

The emphasis on personal freedom in our day, Lord, has denied certain freedoms to those who know you. I ask you to restore the Bible to its central place in schools as the primary book of wisdom and truth. Your Word, O Lord, is right, and all your works are done in truth.[5] Blessed is the nation whose God is you, O Lord.[6]

Bring revival to the schools of our land. I thank you that it is your will for all people to be saved, and to come unto the knowledge of the truth. Lead the students of our land to seek truth, and in so doing, to find that there is one God, and one mediator between God and men — our Lord and Savior Jesus Christ.[7]

Take away the blindness of some of our educators — especially those who have a humanistic orientation — who place their faith in the wisdom of men instead of the power of God.[8]

Many of our institutions of higher learning were originally founded on the solid rock of your Word, O Lord. We claim your promise for these schools, Lord Jesus, your promise that declares that you will restore all things.[9]

Restore to all our schools the purpose and intention of providing the highest possible quality of education while embracing the values and truth of your Word.[10]

Happy is the man who finds your wisdom, Lord, and the man who gains understanding prospers. [11] Teach our children and young people to keep their hearts with all diligence, for out of the heart are the issues of life. Help our young people to return to your Word, to attend to your voice, to incline their ears to your sayings, for they are life unto those who find them, and health to all their flesh. [12]

Renew our minds, Lord, through your Word so that we will learn to see things as you see them. [13] Renew our school systems, Lord, so that they will become centers of righteousness and godliness once again. [14]

References: *(1)Proverbs 15:2; (2)1 Thessalonians 5:15; (3)Psalms 121:7; (4)2 Timothy 2:15; (5)Psalms 33:4; (6)Psalms 33:12; (7)1Timothy 2:4-5; (8)1 Corinthians 2:5; (9)Matthew 17:11; (10)Psalms 119:160; (11)Proverbs 3:13; (12)Proverbs 4:20-23; (13)Romans 12:2; (14)1 Timothy 6:11.*

Our Enemies

Key Thought: Pray for your enemies.

Key Scripture: *"Blessed are they which are persecuted for righteousness' sake: for theirs is the kingdom of heaven. Blessed are ye, when men shall revile you, and persecute you, and shall say all manner of evil against you falsely, for my sake. Rejoice, and be exceeding glad: for great is your reward in heaven.... Love your enemies, bless them that curse you, do good to them that hate you, and pray for them which despitefully use you, and persecute you"* (Matt. 5:10-12,44).

Prayer: Lord, teach us how to overcome evil with good.[1] As much as possible, help us to live in peace with all people.[2] Make us your peacemakers because we know the peacemakers will be called your children.[3] Help me to love my personal enemies and the enemies of our nation whom I now lift up to you: _____

_____ .

Bless them, Father, and help me to learn how to forgive them.[4] Thank you for watching over us throughout the history of our country, through each of the armed conflicts we've faced. I pray, Lord God, that you will keep us from war by giving our leaders the wisdom to deal with our enemies in other ways. When war becomes inevitable, I pray that you will endow our Commander-in-Chief, the Secretary of State, the Secretary of Defense, the Chairman of the Joint Chiefs of Staff and all other officials with the wisdom to know how to defend our nation — and others less fortunate than us — with the greatest of expertise and wisdom.

Even as you told David that you would deliver his enemies into his hands, I pray that you would deliver our enemies into our hands swiftly and speedily when wars and conflicts arise[5] so that the shedding of blood and losses of lives on both sides will be kept low. As your prophet Ezra pointed out, your hand is upon all them who seek you for good, but your power and your wrath are against all those who forsake you.[6] Lord, watch over our servicemen and servicewomen. Draw them unto you. Anoint the chaplains who minister to their needs and may many find you as their personal Savior and Lord.

Keep your hand upon our country, Lord. Deliver us from the hand of our enemies.[7] You have always delivered us, even from strong enemies, Lord, and I beseech you to continue to do so.[8] I thank you that you have given me the shield of your salvation. Your right hand holds me up and your gentleness has made me great.[9]

I ask you for victory over all our enemies, Father, and to help me and the citizens of our country not to gloat when our enemy falls.[10] Thank you for your promise that you will make Jesus' enemies His footstool.[11] Help us always to remember, Lord, that it is you who gives us the victory over our enemies. You teach our hands to war, and our fingers to fight. You are our strength, our goodness, our fortress, our high tower, our deliverer. Lord, you are our shield and you are the One who subdues people under our feet.[12]

References: *(1)Romans 12:21; (2)Hebrews 12:14; (3)Matthew 5:9; (4)Mark 11:26; (5)1 Samuel 24:4; (6)Ezra 8:22; (7)Ezra 8:31; (8)Psalms 18:17; (9)Psalms 18:35; (10)Proverbs 24:17-18; (11)Matthew 22:44; (12)Psalms 144:1-2.*

The Environment

Key Thought: The earth is the Lord's.

Key Scripture: *"In the beginning God created the heaven and the earth. And the earth was without form, and void; and darkness was upon the face of the deep. And the Spirit of God moved upon the face of the waters....And God saw that it was good" (Gen. 1:1-2,25).*

Prayer: O Lord, my God, the heavens declare your glory and the firmament shows forth your handiwork.[1] You form the mountains and create the wind. The Lord of hosts is your name.[2] I thank you that you have created mankind in your own image, and you have declared that it is our responsibility to have dominion over your creation, to replenish the earth and to subdue it.[3] Lord, help all of your creatures to realize that the earth is yours and the fulness thereof.[4] Help us to partake of the fulness you have provided with thanksgiving, to enjoy your creation and to be good stewards of all that you have given to us.

You send forth your Spirit and creation takes place. Renew the face of the earth, Lord. Let your glory endure forever and ever rejoice in your works.[5]

As men and women and children in our land behold the marvelous works that you have done, may they be reminded of who you are and what their response to you should be. You have declared that which may be known of you is made manifest in your creation. I thank you that you reveal your power and your reality through your handiwork. The invisible things about you are clearly seen through your creation. You can be understood through the things that you have made. Your eternal power and Godhead is revealed in nature, Lord; therefore, people are without excuse. May the people of our nation be led to seek you, Lord, as they behold your creation.[6]

You sit upon the circle of the earth. You stretch out the heavens as a curtain and you spread them out as a tent to dwell in. Lead men, Father, to lift up their eyes on high so that they will be able to behold the One who created the environment, for you are strong in power.[7]

Help all Americans to be good stewards of your creation, Father, and of all that you have made. You own the cattle on a thousand hills, all the fowls of the mountains, every beast of the forest, and the wild beasts of the fields.[8] May I never make the mistake of thinking that anything you've given is my own personal possession.

Forgive us, Lord, for the ways in which we have abused the natural resources you have provided for us. The people of your creation have polluted the air and water with chemicals, we've improperly depleted the earth of vital elements and some species of wildlife — we have done great damage to much of your beautiful work. Forgive us, Father, and help us to bring the environment into a state of recovery. Unite us in this common goal, Father. May those people who know your name take the leadership in this important work of restoration and recovery.

Father, give us wisdom[9] regarding how to properly manage your creation, and let the wisdom you give produce a consensus and unity in the hearts and minds of our people[10] that will enable us to take the necessary actions to properly use, protect and preserve our environment.

Lord Jesus, by you were all things created.[11] You are worthy to receive glory and honor and power.[12] You have made your wonderful works to be remembered, and you are gracious and full of compassion.[13]

References: *(1)Psalms 19:1; (2)Amos 4:13; (3)Genesis 1:26; (4)Psalms 24:1; (5)Psalms 104:30-31; (6)Romans 1:19-20; (7)Isaiah 40:22,26; (8)Psalms 50:11; (9)James 3:17; (10)Psalms 133:1-3; (11)Colossians 1:16-17; (12)Revelation 4:11; (13)Psalms 111:3-4.*

Fear

Key Thought: Satan tries to control mankind through fear.

Key Scripture: *"I sought the Lord, and he heard me, and delivered me from all my fears"* *(Ps. 34:4).*

Prayer: Heavenly Father, I thank you that you have provided the perfect antidote for fear — faith in your Son, the Lord Jesus Christ. Lead men, women and young people in our nation to a saving faith that will dispell all their fears.[1]

Lord, become the light and salvation of the United States. Lead people to acknowledge you as the strength of their lives and deliver them from fear.[2] When fear comes, lead men, women and young people to seek you, Lord; help them to know that you are hearing their prayers and you are delivering them from all their fears.[3]

I pray specifically for _____ _____ who is/are currently victimized by fear. Help him/her/them to know that your name is a strong tower into which the righteous may run and be forever safe.[4] Let him/her/them know that they need not be afraid for the terror by night; nor for the arrow that flies by day because you are with him/her/them.[5]

Strengthen the people of our nation, Father, so that they will not fear. Deliver them from the dismay of darkness. You are our God; we are one nation under you and you have promised to help us. Thank you, Lord. Uphold this country with the right hand of your righteousness.[6]

Father, in the mighty name of Jesus, I come against the stronghold of fear that Satan is using to control and defeat my fellow-Americans. I rebuke that spirit of fear in the power of your blood, and I ask you to deliver this nation from its bondage to fear.[7] Lord, you are so faithful to us, and you have promised to establish us and to keep us from all evil.[8] Accomplish this in the United States of America, I pray.

Thank you for your love in which there is no fear. Your perfect love casts out all fear.[9] Praise your name.

References: (1)Isaiah 12:2; (2)Psalms 27:1; (3)Psalms 34:4; (4)Proverbs 18:10; (5)Psalm 91:5; (6)Isaiah 41:10; (7)Romans 8:15; (8)2 Thessalonians 3:3; (9)1 John 4:18.

Our Forefathers

Key Thought: "Our fathers brought forth, upon this continent, a new nation, conceived in Liberty, and dedicated to the proposition that all men are created equal" (Abraham Lincoln).

Key Scripture: *"And Moses called all Israel, and said unto them, Hear, O Israel, the statutes and judgments which I speak in your ears this day, that ye may learn them, and keep, and do them. The Lord our God made a covenant with us in Horeb. The Lord made not this covenant with our fathers, but with us, even us, who are all of us here alive this day" (Deut. 5:1-3).*

Prayer: Lord God, when you spoke to Abram you promised that your covenant was with him and you told him that you would make him a father of many nations.[1] When you spoke to Jacob, you promised that in his seed all the families of the earth would be blessed.[2] I thank you that you are the God of Abraham, the God of Isaac and the God of Jacob, and you are the God of the fathers of our nation as well.[3] Thank you for our forefathers who paved the way for us in the development of the United States.

Father, as I remember all those who went before — the patriarchs of the Old Testament, your disciples in the New Testament and the founders of our nation, I am filled with gratitude for all you have done in and through them to provide us the freedom to worship you in spirit and in truth.[4]

As I ponder the accomplishments of our forefathers, I am reminded, Lord, that you are not the God of the dead, but of the living.[5] In the same way that Elisha sought a double portion of Elijah's spirit to be upon him,[6] I ask you to pour out your Spirit in full measure upon our nation, Lord.[7] Lead multitudes within our nation to call upon you for deliverance.

Thank you for hearing and answering the prayers of our forefathers. Your wonderful promise remains ever true: "Blessed is the man that feareth you, Lord. His seed shall be mighty upon the earth, and the generation of the upright shall be blessed."[8] May this present generation of Americans become "the generation of the upright."[9] May it be said of us in this generation, "And they became a blessed nation because God was their Lord."[10] Help us as a nation to revere the traditional values set forth in your Word and adhered to by our forefathers.

Lord, you are so good to us. You have always been a stronghold in the day of trouble.[11] Thank you for the courage of our forefathers — they were swifter than eagles and stronger than lions.[12] Help our nation to regain that ideal of courage in our present day. Show our people the importance of being strong in you and in the power of your might.[13]

Thank you, Father, for the covenant you established with our forefathers. Because of your dealings in their lives, I know you will never forsake us nor destroy us nor forget your covenant with your people.[14] I thank you for the New Covenant you have given to us, Lord Jesus, and you have sealed it with your own precious blood. Thank you for shedding your blood for the remission of sins.[15]

Father, I pray for the people of America, that they would accept Jesus Christ as their personal Lord and Savior, and be cleansed by His blood.[16]

References: (1)*Genesis 17:4;* (2)*Genesis 28:14;* (3)*Exodus 3:6;*
(4)*John 4:24;* (5)*Mark 12:27;* (6)*2 Kings 2:9;* (7)*Joel 2:28;*
(8)*Psalms 112:1-2;* (9)*Psalms 112:2;* (10)*Psalms 33:12;*
(11)*Nahum 1:7;* (12)*2 Samuel 1:23;* (13)*Ephesians 6:10;*
(14)*Deuteronomy 4:31;* (15)*Matthew 26:28;* (16)*1 John 1:7.*

Freedom

Key Thought: Freedom and duty go hand in hand.

Key Scripture: *"Stand fast therefore in the liberty wherewith Christ hath made us free, and be not entangled again with the yoke of bondage"* (Gal. 5:1).

Prayer: Thank you, heavenly Father, for the United States of America, and for the freedoms, liberties and rights we enjoy as citizens of this blessed country. Help the people of our nation to cherish these freedoms and never to take them lightly. To always remember that they were provided at great cost, including the loss of many lives of servicemen and servicewomen.

In the same way, Lord Jesus, you have provided spiritual freedom to all those who come to you by faith.[1]

I thank you for the freedom of religion, press, assembly, speech, the right to bear arms and all the other rights and liberties I enjoy as a citizen of this great country. May the people of America never abuse any of these rights and privileges of citizenship, and help each of us, Father, to always do our part to keep our country good and strong. Lead us in paths of righteousness for your name's sake.[2]

Thank you, Father, for your promise that we will know the truth and the truth will make us free. When you give freedom to your children, we are set free indeed.[3] Teach the citizens of our country that all true freedom comes from submission to the Lordship of your Son. Thank you for the founding fathers who established "one country under God." Help us to honor all people, to love one another, and to reverence and to honor the president.[4]

Father, pour forth your Spirit upon our land in special grace and power so that multitudes will be saved.[5] Bless our country with a year of Jubilee — a time when you will proclaim liberty throughout the land because the people walk in holiness before you.[6] I ask you to proclaim liberty to all those who are oppressed,[7] to cause the gospel to be preached to the poor, to heal the brokenhearted and bring deliverance to the captives, recovering of sight to the blind, and set at liberty those who are bruised.[8] Help people everywhere to know that you deliver people from the bondage of corruption into the glorious liberty of your children.[9]

Thank you for calling us unto liberty through Jesus Christ.[10] Help us always to look into your perfect law of liberty (your Word) and to continue therein. To be doers of your Word who are continually blessed.[11]

Great is your faithfulness, O God, my Father.[12] Your faithfulness is unto all generations; you have established the earth according to your principles.[13] Thank you for your faithfulness to the United States of America.

References: *(1)Ephesians 1:6-9; (2)Psalms 23:3; (3)John 8:32,36; (4)1 Peter 2:13-17; (5)Joel 2:28; (6)Leviticus 25:10; (7)Jeremiah 34:8; (8)Luke 4:18; (9)Romans 8:21; (10)Galatians 5:13; (11)James 1:22; (12)Lamentations 3:23; (13)Psalms 119:90-91.*

The Future of Our Land

Key Thought: The end of the story is already revealed! Jesus is coming again!

Key Scripture: *"And we desire that every one of you do shew the same diligence to the full assurance of hope unto the end: That ye be not slothful, but followers of them who through faith and patience inherit the promises"* (Heb. 6:11-12).

Prayer: Heavenly Father, I come to you now in behalf of the United States of America. You are the author and finisher of our faith,[1] Lord, and I know that you will complete the work you have begun in our nation. You have many purposes for our country to fulfill, and I know you will perform your work in and through our country[2] until the day of your return.

Thank you for your faithfulness,[3] your goodness[4] and your mercy,[5] Lord God. Watch over our nation and fulfill your promises to us and to the generations to come. Teach our people that all of your promises are *yes* in Christ.[6] Your faithfulness is unto all generations; you have established the earth, and it abides.[7] Teach us your way, O Lord, and lead us in a plain path because of our enemies. Deliver our country from the will of our enemies. I believe to see your goodness revealed in the land of the living.[8]

Father, you know the plans you have for us, plans to prosper us and not to harm us, plans to give us hope and a future. Thank you for your promise that when we call upon you that you will listen. And that we will find you when we seek you with all our heart. I ask you to stir the hearts of all Americans to seek you with all their hearts, to call upon you and to enter into the plan and the future that you have for us.[9]

Let your mercy be upon us, O Lord, according as we hope in you.[10] Stay your hand of judgment from our land, Lord, for there are still many righteous citizens who are faithful to you and there are still many lost to be saved.[11]

Blessed is the nation whose God is you, O Lord.[12] Hear the prayers of your people, and bring revival to our land. I pray for all those who do not know you, Lord, for they are aliens from your land of promise and strangers from your covenant. Such people cannot know hope because they are in the world without you.[13] Lead the people of our country who do not know you to salvation through faith in Jesus Christ.[14]

As your church in America looks forward to the blessed hope — the glorious appearing of Jesus — I ask, O Lord, that you would keep us pure. May we never forget how you gave yourself for us to redeem us from all iniquity. Purify us unto yourself as a peculiar people, zealous of good works.[15]

Impart your blessing to this generation, and to all generations yet to come. Be with our children, our grandchildren and with all who come after us. Teach us to intercede in prayer for our friends and our enemies, and as we do so, heavenly Father, I ask you to bless the latter days of America even more than you have blessed the former days.[16]

References: *(1)Hebrews 12:2; (2)Philippians 1:6; (3)Psalms 119:90; (4)Psalms 27:13; (5)Psalms 56:1; (6)2 Corinthians 1:20; (7)Psalms 119:90; (8)Psalms 27:11-13; (9)Jeremiah 29:11-13; (10)Psalms 33:22; (11)2 Peter 2:6-8; (12)Psalms 33:12; (13)Ephesians 2:12; (14)John 3:16; (15)Titus 2:13-14; (16)Job 42:10-12.*

Gender Gap

Key Thought: God judges men and women by their hearts.

Key Scripture: *"There is neither Jew nor Greek, there is neither bond nor free, there is neither male nor female: for ye are all one in Christ Jesus"* *(Gal. 3:28).*

Prayer: Lord Jesus Christ, Son of God, how I thank you that your Word provides so many answers to the individual and social dilemmas of our time. I look to your Word for the wisdom and understanding I need to pray for our nation.

Lord, there is prejudice, discrimination and animosity among various groups within our country. Sometimes strong feelings of enmity even divide men from women. I know this is not your will for our people for you have abolished enmity through your death on the cross.[1] Heavenly Father, you are our peace and you are able to bring unity to our land. Break down the middle wall of partition that divides the genders and reconcile both groups unto you in one body through your cross.[2]

Lord God, all things are of you. Thank you for reconciling me to yourself, and thank you for giving me the ministry of reconciliation.[3] Help me to become a minister of reconciliation whenever I see divisions among men and women.

Help the people of the United States to see that through you we can learn to submit ourselves to one another. Through fearing and honoring you, Lord, we are able to learn how to relate to all others.[4]

Teach us your way, Lord, so that we will know how to walk in your paths.[5] Your precious Word teaches us to speak the same thing so that there be no divisions among us. You want us to be perfectly joined together in the same mind and in the same judgment.[6] Father, I pray in the name of Jesus that you would[7] bring this to pass in our land.

Restore spiritual values to our nation, Lord. Show our people that so much of the extremism we see around us stems from a carnal mind-set. Wherever there is envying and strife and divisions, you have pointed out that a carnal attitude is at work.[8] Help me and the people of our nation, especially the people of your body, Lord, to remember that to be carnally minded is death but to be spiritually minded is life and peace.[9]

Come against all strongholds of darkness in those who walk in the vanity of their minds, having their understanding darkened, being alienated from your life through their ignorance and the blindness of their hearts.[10] Teach men and women to be tender-hearted to one another and forgiving in their attitudes toward each other.[11] Help men and women to see that they are not in competition with one another, but they can work together for the common good.

Lord, you have been favorable unto our land. Forgive the iniquity of our people; cover all our sin. Take away all your wrath and turn us, O God of our salvation. Revive us again so that the people of our land will once more rejoice in you, putting aside their differences and focusing on you and your glory. Let your truth spring out of the earth and your righteousness come down from heaven.[12]

Help those who are involved in the gender gap to remember that you made us to differ from one another. Remind us all that who we are and what we have were designed by you for special purposes. Teach us to be content with who we are and what we have been given.[13]

The wisdom of this world is foolishness to you, O Lord. Everything is yours, Lord.[14] Bring healing to the gender gap in our nation, and set men and women free to serve you.

References: (1)Ephesians 2:14-15; (2)Ephesians 2:16; (3)2 Corinthians 5:18; (4)Ephesians 5:21; (5)Psalms 86:11; (6)1 Corinthians 1:10; (7)John 16:23; (8)1 Corinthians 3:3; (9)Romans 8:6; (10)Ephesians 4:17-18; (11)Ephesians 4:32; (12)Psalms 85; (13)Hebrews 13:5; (14)1 Corinthians 3:18-22.

Generation Gap

Key Thought: The human spirit never ages.

Key Scripture: *"See, I will send you the prophet Elijah before that great and dreadful day of the Lord comes. He will turn the hearts of the fathers to their children, and the hearts of the children to their fathers; or else I will come and strike the land with a curse"* *(Mal. 4:5-6, NIV).*

Prayer: Dear Father, I come to you now in behalf of the generations who dwell in the United States of America. I beseech you to send forth your Holy Spirit and fulfill your promise to turn the hearts of the younger generations to the older generations, and the hearts of the older generations to the younger. I implore you to accomplish this miracle in our midst so that it will not be necessary for you to strike our land with a curse. I ask you this, trusting in your love and your mercy.[1]

Throughout both testaments of your Word, Father, you have shown us the importance of strong relationships being encouraged and developed between the young and the old. Help me to foster such strong relationships with people of all ages. Lord, make your name to be remembered in all the generations of our nation so that people will learn to praise you forever and ever.[2]

Draw forth your people, the sheep of your pasture; may their songs of salvation and thanksgiving be heard throughout our land. Lead me and all your people to show forth your praise to all generations.[3]

Help us all to see that agism is another form of prejudicial discrimination that you abhor because it is sinful. I thank you, loving Father, that you do not look upon the outward appearance (or upon a person's age); rather, you look upon a person's heart.[4] Teach the young not to judge the old and teach the old not to judge the young. Remind us all, Father, that you will judge us with the same standard by which we judge others.[5]

In your kingdom, Lord, people of all ages are invited to serve you freely and fully. Praise your name that age is not a factor in your service. Your faithfulness, Lord God, is unto all generations.[6]

You, Lord, are the first and the last. You are calling all the generations to follow you.[7] Restore to our land the high value your Word places upon honor, respect and dignity. Give our young people teachable hearts to respond positively to being trained up in the way they should go[8] and to honor the elderly,[9] and may the older generations endeavor to understand and love the younger with patience.[10]

Lord, you declared that David died "in good old age," and that he died with honor.[11] May our society once again regard old age as good and honorable and may we learn to respect the wisdom and knowledge acquired through the years by our elderly citizens. When I enter the years of seniorhood, help me to remember that you have declared that the hoary head is a crown of glory, if it be found in the way of righteousness.[12]

Draw the young people in our land to remember you and to love you, their Creator, in the days of their youth even when things are going well for them.[13] Give them no rest until they say yes to you. Lord Jesus, you are our peace. You are able to make both generations one in their desire and zeal to follow you. Break down the walls of partition and hostility between the generations and reconcile both unto yourself in one body by the cross. I thank you that you have already slain the enmity between the generations by your death on the cross.[14]

Lord God omnipotent, you are in charge of our country. You are the One who reigns over all.[15] Continue to reign in our land. Show all the generations how to be glad and to rejoice and to give honor unto you, for the Marriage of the Lamb is coming and on that blessed day the differences in our ages will pale to insignificance because all that will matter is you, O Lord.[16] Hasten that day, precious Savior.

References: *(1)Psalms 52:8; (2)Psalms 45:17; (3)Psalms 79:13; (4)1 Samuel 16:7; (5)Matthew 7:1-2; (6)Psalms 119:90; (7)Isaiah 41:4; (8)Proverbs 22:6; (9)Leviticus 19:32; (10)James 1:4; (11)1 Chronicles 29:28; (12)Proverbs 16:31; (13)Ecclesiastes 12:1; (14)Ephesians 2:14-16; (15)Revelation 19:6; (16)Revelation 19:7.*

God's Merciful Judgment

Key Thought: Justice and mercy go hand in hand.

Key Scripture: *"Thou hast a mighty arm: strong is thy hand, and high is thy right hand. Justice and judgment are the habitation of thy throne: mercy and truth shall go before thy face. Blessed is the people that know the joyful sound: they shall walk, O Lord, in the light of thy countenance"* *(Ps. 89:13-15).*

Prayer: Lord, you have been our dwelling place in all generations. Before the mountains were brought forth, before you had formed the earth and the world, even from everlasting to everlasting, you are God.[1] You are the very habitation of justice, and you are the hope of our fathers.[2] Justice and judgment are the habitation of your glorious throne.[3]

I beseech you, most just and merciful Father, to let your mercy prevail in our land during this difficult hour of history. Have mercy on us. Have mercy on us. Have mercy on us.[4]

Your way is to do justice and judgment, O Lord.[5] Help our people to always honor your Word and to follow your ways. As you pointed out to the people of Israel, Father, it is your desire for our leaders to remove violence, spoil and oppression from our land. You want all in leadership to execute justice and judgment and to have a just balance.[6] Help our leaders to be very responsive to these important needs, and to be fair to all people.

I pray for the officials and courts of our country who have the responsibility for executing your justice, mercy and judgment. Lord, fill them with wisdom and help them to approach all people with impartiality. I thank you, Father, that you are no respector of persons.[7] Help them and all Americans to do justly, and to love mercy, and to walk humbly with you.[8]

Your immutable Word declares that in every nation he who fears you and works righteousness is accepted by you.[9] I thank you that you love me and that you have loved me with everlasting love. I pray that you will draw the people of America with the same lovingkindness that drew me to you.[10] In your amazing mercy, it is not your will that anyone should perish, and you are not slack concerning your promise. Rather, Lord, you are longsuffering toward mankind, and you want all people to come to repentance.[11] How I thank you and praise you that you temper your judgment with mercy and love.

Father, because of your great love you sent Jesus to die for us[12] and to save us from wrath.[13] Let the Word of your gospel come with great power to America.[14] Let that word be like a fire, Lord, and like a hammer that breaks a rock into pieces.[15] I pray in Jesus' name that the overwhelming majority of Americans will respond to your Word and receive Jesus Christ as their Lord.[16]

The increase of your government shall never end; praise you, God! You are establishing, building and ordering your kingdom, O Lord, and it is being built with judgment and mercy that will last forevermore. I thank you that your zeal will bring this to pass.[17] Be zealous for America, Lord, and shower her with your grace, mercy and peace.[18]

References: (1)Psalms 90:1-2; (2)Jeremiah 50:7; (3)Psalms 89:14; (4)Psalms 123:3; (5)Genesis 18:19; (6)Ezekiel 45:9-10; (7)Acts 10:34; (8)Micah 6:8; (9)Acts 10:35; (10)Jeremiah 31:3; (11)2 Peter 3:9; (12)Romans 5:8; (13)Romans 5:9; (14)Hebrews 4:12; (15)Jeremiah 23:29; (16)John 1:12; (17)Isaiah 9:7; (18)1 Timothy 1:2.

Homosexuality

Key Thought: Jesus is the answer, no matter what the question.

Key Scripture: *"For this cause God gave them up unto vile affections: for even their women did change the natural use into that which is against nature: And likewise also the men, leaving the natural use of the woman, burned in their lust one toward another; men with men working that which is unseemly, and receiving in themselves that recompence of their error which was meet"* *(Rom. 1:26-27).*

Prayer: Heavenly Father, I thank you that you are love[1] and that if we will learn to seek first your kingdom and your righteousness all the things we need will be added unto us.[2] Reveal these dynamic, life-changing truths to the homosexuals in our land. Help them to realize that their sexual orientation is a form of idolatry,[3] and that you will have no other gods before you.[4]

A spirit of homosexuality grips the hearts of many men, women and young people in the age in which we live. Set them free, Father.[5] Help them to flee youthful lusts,[6] to turn away from ungodliness,[7] to see that fornication is sin,[8] to recognize the beauty of holiness[9] and to realize that Jesus is the way, the truth and the life.[10]

Father, in the authority of the name of Jesus,[11] I come against the blinding influence of the prince of darkness[12] who seeks to destroy[13] many people in our country through homosexuality, the lust of the flesh, the lust of the eyes and the pride of life.[14] I proclaim liberty to these captives,[15] for this is your will for them.

Grant the homosexuals of our land a spirit of wisdom and revelation in the knowledge of you that their understanding may be enlightened.[16] Eph 1:17-18

Send your Word to them through anointed believers.[17] Give them hearing ears [18] and hearts open to receive your Word.[19] Grace them with godly sorrow that produces repentance [20] As you draw them by your Spirit, Father,[21] may they truly repent of their sins, turn to you[22] and receive Jesus Christ as their Savior,[23] Lord[24] and Deliverer[25].

Lord, speak to the heart of _____ _____ who suffer(s) from the deception of homosexuality. Set him/her/them free, Lord Jesus. Let him/her/them know how much you love him/her/them.

Equip your Church, heavenly Father, with the compassion and strength and wisdom we need to minister to those who struggle with homosexuality. Help us to hold onto the truth that we can love the sinner, as you do, even though we hate the sin, as you do. Help your Church to restore hope to homosexuals by showing them that your way is perfect and your Word is tried. Your Word, O Father, is a mighty buckler to all who put their trust in you.[26]

Through faith in your name, Lord Jesus, the homosexual, like all of us, is made strong. Pour forth your Spirit on those who have traded their gender identities for a lie, give them the faith to lay hold of your promises, for I know this will lead them to the perfect soundness, health and happiness that comes through faith in your name.[27]

References: (1)1 John 4:8; (2)Matthew 6:33; (3)Romans 1:23; (4)Exodus 34:14; (5)Galatians 5:1; (6)2 Timothy 2:22; (7)Romans 11:26; (8)1 Corinthians 6:18; (9)Psalms 110:3; (10)John 14:6; (11)Mark 16:17; (12)Luke 10:19; (13)John 10:10; (14)1 John 2:16; (15)Jeremiah 34:8; (16)Ephesians 1:17-18; (17)Matthew 28:19-20; (18)Matthew 11:15; (19)Mark 4:20; (20)2 Corinthians 7:10; (21)1 Corinthians 12:3; (22)Acts 2:38; (23)1 John 4:14; (24)Romans 10:13; (25)Psalms 18:2; (26)Psalms 18:30; (27)1 John 5:13.

Hopelessness

Key Thought: Hope is an anchor for the soul.

Key Scripture: *"Deliver me, O my God, out of the hand of the wicked, out of the hand of the unrighteous and cruel man. For thou art my hope, O Lord God; thou art my trust from my youth"* (Ps. 71:4-5).

Prayer: Dear Father, keep your Church in America and around the world from not being moved away from the hope your gospel affords to all who put their trust in you.[1] Show the people of our nation that the true answer to their problems is found in your most gracious invitation: "I will give unto him that is athirst of the fountain of the water of life freely."[2]

Lord, many in our land live in fear and hopelessness. I pray for them now as I ask you to fill their hearts with peace and to restore their hope. There is no need to fear when we place our hope and trust in you and in your Word for you have promised to remain with us.[3] We have no reason to be dismayed when you are our God.[4] You have promised to become our hope even in the day of evil.[5] Make the people of our land "prisoners of hope" because they place their trust in you.[6]

Heavenly Father, your Word tells us that Jesus is our only hope.[7] Show this clearly to the people of our nation, young and old. I pray for my fellow citizens that they would commit their lives to Jesus Christ as Savior and Lord and lay hold onto the hope which you give to all who come to you in faith.[8]

Out of the depths I cry unto you, O Lord, in behalf of all those who are hopeless in our land.[9] Bring their souls out of prison that they might be able to praise your name.[10] I pray now for _____

_____ who feels hopeless because of

_____ . Restore hope to him/her/them as he/she/they learn to call upon your name. May he/she/they hear your Word and be glad. Put gladness in his/her/their heart(s).[11]

For the people of the United States of America I pray, Lord, and I ask you to help them to fully realize that he who comes unto you shall never hunger, and he that believes on you shall never thirst.[12] You are the God of all hope.[13]

References: *(1)Colossians 1:23; (2)Revelation 21:6; (3)Hebrews 13:5-6; (4)Isaiah 41:10; (5)Jeremiah 17:17; (6)Zechariah 9:12; (7)1 Timothy 1:1; (8)Hebrews 6:18; (9)Psalms 130:1; (10)Psalms 142:7; (11)Psalms 4:7; (12)John 6:35; (13)Romans 15:13.*

Idolatry

Key Thought: Anything that takes our eyes off of Jesus causes problems in our lives.

Key Scripture: *"Then shall ye call upon me, and ye shall go and pray unto me, and I will hearken unto you. And ye shall seek me, and find me, when ye shall search for me with all your heart"* (Jer. 29:12-13).

Prayer: Lord, you are the one, true God, and I thank you that you will not permit your people to have any other gods before you.[1] Reveal to this idolatrous generation that we must flee from idolatry[2] by seeking you and your righteousness first of all.[3]

I thank you for Jesus, Father, and I am so grateful that it pleased you to let all fulness dwell in Him.[4] Many in our nation are alienated from you because of their wicked works, and I beseech you to reconcile them unto yourself.[5] Grant them the grace of godly sorrow that will produce repentance in them unto salvation.[6]

Lord God, constrain our people from forsaking you to serve other gods as so many are doing today.[7] Many do not hearken unto the leaders and ministers you have provided and they leave the safety of your love to go after other gods.[8] Lord God, have mercy upon our nation. Yes, Lord, have mercy upon us.[9]

Our land is polluted with the blood of evildoers.[10] We need your grace in this crucial hour, Father. Make all the idolaters in our nation be greatly ashamed.[11] Give them no rest, day or night, until they have repented and therefore find their rest in you.[12]

I pray now for _____ who trusts in the false idol of _____ _____ instead of in you. Deliver him/her/them from bondage and set them free from his/her/their blindness so that he/she/they will be able to place his/her/their total trust in you.

Father, there are idols in our land and in the hearts of our people. I implore you to break through to this stubborn and rebellious generation.[13] Do whatever is necessary to help present-day idolaters to see their sin, how it grieves your heart and how their idolatry relates to the abundant evil of our day.

O God, you demonstrate your justice and your mercy as you pour out your fury upon the heathen who willingly turn away from you and upon the families who do not call on your name.[14] In your mercy, bring them the word of the gospel to open their eyes, and turn them from darkness to light and from the power of Satan unto you.[15] I pray for them and I cry out, "deliver these souls from darkness, Father, and may they ever turn from their wickedness." May they see the error of their ways and humble themselves,[16] call upon the Lord and be saved.[17] Great is your mercy, O God.[18]

References: *(1)Exodus 20:3; (2)1 Corinthians 10:14; (3)Matthew 6:33; (4)Colossians 1:19; (5)Colossians 1:21; (6)2 Corinthians 7:10; (7)Joshua 24:16; (8)Judges 2:17; (9)Psalms 6:2; (10)Psalms 106:38; (11)Isaiah 42:17; (12)Revelation 14:11; (13)Psalms 78:8; (14)Jeremiah 10:25; (15)Acts 26:18; (16)James 4:10; (17)Romans 10:13; (18)Psalms 57:10.*

The Incarcerated

Key Thought: God loves prisoners and He wants them to turn to Him.

Key Scripture: *"For I was an hungred, and ye gave me meat: I was thirsty, and ye gave me drink: I was a stranger, and ye took me in: Naked, and ye clothed me: I was sick, and ye visited me: I was in prison and ye came unto me. Then shall the righteous answer him, saying, Lord, when saw we thee an hungred, and fed thee? or thirsty, and gave thee drink? When saw we thee a stranger, and took thee in? or naked, and clothed thee? Or when saw we thee sick, or in prison, and came unto thee? And the King shall answer and say unto them, Verily I say unto you, Inasmuch as ye have done it unto one of the least of these my brethren, ye have done it unto me"* (Matt. 25:35-40).

Prayer: Lord, thank you for reminding me of my need to pray for and visit prisoners — men and women who have lost their freedoms because they have committed crimes, and some who are confined even though they have not done wrong. Lead all prisoners unto yourself and lead many believers to go into the prisons of our nation to hold forth your Word of life to those who sit in darkness.[1]

Anoint the chaplains and other clergy who minister to the prisoners of our nation. Help them to lead the men and women in our jails and prisons out of darkness into your marvelous light.[2] Thank you, Lord, for hearing the poor, and not despising the prisoners.[3]

145

I thank you that you have called me and my brothers and sisters to be a light to those who sit in darkness, to open the blind eyes, to bring out the prisoners from the prison, and them that sit in darkness out of the prison house.[4] Protect those prisoners who know you personally, Lord, and set those free who have earned their freedom. For the others, Father, I ask that you would draw them by your Spirit to find spiritual freedom through the newness of life you offer to all through faith in Jesus Christ our Lord.[5]

Let the sighing of the prisoner come before you, O Lord. According to the greatness of your power preserve those who are appointed to die — the prisoners awaiting execution on the death rows of our land.[6] I thank you that you are looking down from the height of your sanctuary in heaven, and you are beholding the earth. You hear the groaning of the prisoner and you care about those who are appointed to die.[7] Thank you for your grace and saving love, dear Father.

Lord Jesus, I praise you that you have once suffered for the sins of the world, the just for the unjust, that you might bring us all to the Father, being put to death in the flesh, but quickened by the Spirit. By that same Spirit you went and preached to the spirits in prison which sometimes were disobedient and you redeemed many.[8]

Father, I ask that you would send your Spirit to bring conviction and repentance to the prisoners of our land, that you would indeed send a revival to the prisoners and turn the prisons into churches and temples of your radiant glory and presence.

Have mercy on the prisoners, Lord, according to your lovingkindness, according to your tender mercies, blot out

their transgressions. Wash them thoroughly from their
iniquity and cleanse them from their sin. Lead them to
acknowledge their transgressions so that they will
recognize that they have sinned against you.[9] Let your
goodness lead them to repentance[10] and to receive newness
of life through Jesus Christ[11] and to serve you in newness
of spirit.[12] Amen.

References: (1)Philippians 2:16; (2)1 Peter 2:9; (3)Psalms
69:33; (4)Isaiah 42:6-7; (5)Romans 6:4; (6)Psalms 79:11;
(7)Psalms 102:19-20; (8)1 Peter 3:19-20; (9)Psalms 51:1-4;
(10)Romans 2:4; (11)Romans 6:4; (12)Romans 7:6.

Intercessors

Key Thought: The front-line soldiers in spiritual combat are the intercessors.

Key Scripture: *"We then that are strong ought to bear the infirmities of the weak, and not to please ourselves"* *(Rom. 15:1).*

Prayer: Heavenly Father, I thank you that you are calling for intercessors in our land today. Draw many believers into this important ministry in behalf of our country, your Church and the world.

Fill your people with your Spirit so that we will be able to rebuild the old waste places. Raise up the foundations of many generations, Lord, for you are the repairer of the breach and you are the restorer of paths to dwell in.[1] Your precious Holy Spirit helps us in our infirmities, for we do not know what we should pray for as we ought, but your Spirit makes intercession for us with groanings that cannot be uttered. Help us to find the mind of your Spirit as we learn to make intercession for our nation and the saints of your Church according to your will.[2]

Teach us how to bear one another's burdens through intercessory prayer so that we will be able to fulfill your law, Lord.[3] As Aaron stood between the dead and the living so that the plague would be stayed, cause many to stand with the company of your intercessors in behalf of

America today.[4] Pour forth your spirit of intercession upon the church in America, Lord, so that believers would be able to inquire of you in behalf of the people.[5] Give them your heart of compassion for the lost and for those trapped in sin.

Thank you for making intercession for us, Lord Jesus, at the right hand of our Father in heaven.[6] I thank you for the certain knowledge that if any man sin, we have you as our advocate with the Father.[7] There is one God, and you, Lord Jesus Christ, are the one mediator between our Father and us.[8] Teach us to pray and show us how to pray.[9]

Father, give your people the heart of Samuel who realized the importance of intercessory prayer when he said, "God forbid that I should sin against the Lord in ceasing to pray for you."[10] Let your ear now be attentive to the needs of our nation and let your eyes be open, Father.[11] I cry unto you in behalf of America today. Raise up your intercessors in our land.

Heavenly Father, I now intercede on behalf of

who you have called to the ministry of intercessory prayer. Help them to realize the vital importance of their ministry and protect them and their families from all harm.[12] Let your Holy Spirit guide them,[13] strengthen them[14] and comfort them[15] as they go forth in warfare for you.[16]

Grant not, O Lord, the desires of the wicked.[17] You are far from the wicked but you hear the prayer of the righteous.[18] O my God, incline your ear and hear the prayers of your people. Open your eyes and behold the desolation of our land. We do not present our supplications before you in our own righteousness, but simply because we know of your great mercies.[19] O Lord, hear; O Lord, forgive; O Lord, hearken and do. Defer not, for your own sake, O my God, for your people are called by your name.[20]

Your eyes are over the righteous and your ears are open to our prayers.[21] Thank you, Father. I receive strength from your promise that the effectual, fervent prayer of a righteous person will always avail much.[22] Bless the United States of America.

References: (1)Isaiah 58:12; (2)Romans 8:26-27; (3)Galatians 6:2; (4)Numbers 16:48; (5)2 Kings 22:13; (6)Hebrews 7:25; (7)1 John 2:1; (8)1 Timothy 2:5; (9)Luke 11:1; (10)1 Samuel 12:23; (11)Nehemiah 1:6; (12)Psalms 91; (13)John 16:13; (14)1 Peter 5:10; (15)Acts 9:31; (16)2 Corinthians 10:4; (17)Psalms 140:8; (18)Prov. 15:29; (19)Daniel 9:18; (20)Daniel 9:19; (21)1 Peter 3:12; (22)James 5:16.

Justice in the Land

Key Thought: "Justice and judgment are the habitation of thy throne: mercy and truth shall go before thy face" (Ps. 89:14).

Key Scripture: *"To do justice and judgment is more acceptable to the Lord than sacrifice" (Prov. 21:3).*

Prayer: O Lord, my heart is fixed; I will sing and give praise, even with my glory. I will praise thee, O Lord, among the people, and I will sing praises unto thee among the nations.[1]

It is my desire, Father, to be like Abraham who knew you and taught his children to keep your ways. Your way is to do justice and judgment, to treat your people with fairness and mercy, that your will might be fulfilled.[2]

Lord, we live in a time when people cry for justice, an era in which there is a great need for deep, spiritual wisdom to be imparted to all our leaders. I pray for the Supreme Court justices, and for all who interpret the laws of our country, that you would imbue them with wisdom from on high.[3]

Father, give us leaders, judges and officers who will judge with a pervading sense of godly and righteous justice. May they never wrest judgment, show improper favor to special interests or take gifts or bribes to influence their decisions. Rather, Lord, lead them to follow that which is altogether just and righteous so that your people will be able to inherit the land which you have given to us.[4]

Bless our land with your presence, Lord, so that all Americans would strive to be just, in the reverent fear of you.[5] Help us to be just in all our dealings with others for the mouth of the just brings forth wisdom. May we never forget that the tongue of the just is as choice silver in your sight, O Lord.[6]

Father, make it plain to the inhabitants of America that the wicked are snared by the transgression of their lips, but the just will be delivered out of trouble.[7]

Justice is supremely important to you, Lord. You have declared that the just or righteous man walks in his integrity, and his children are blessed after him.[8] Lord, give each of our citizens the desire to be known as a just person who walks in integrity. Bless them with this constant desire and with the capacity to walk in integrity.

Lord, you are completely just and you are in the midst of our land. Those who do not follow you do not know the meaning of shame.[9] Draw the unjust to your grace, mercy and truth; convict them of their sin.

Reveal to our nation the wisdom of your Word. I look unto you, and I wait for you, O God of my salvation. I know you hear me, Lord.[10] Show us what you require of us and reveal what is good. Help all Americans to know your will, Father, that you require them to do justly, and to love mercy, and to walk humbly with you.[11] Thank you for hearing my prayer and for pouring forth justice on our land.

References: (1)Psalms 108:1; (2)Genesis 18:19; (3)James 3:17-18; (4)Deuteronomy 16:18-20; (5)2 Samuel 23:3; (6)Proverbs 10:31; (7)Proverbs 12:13; (8)Proverbs 20:7; (9)Zephaniah 3:5; (10)Micah 7:7; (11)Micah 6:8.

Law Enforcement Officials

Key Thought: The law is for the unjust.

Key Scripture: *"For he is the minister of God to thee for good. But if thou do that which is evil, be afraid: for he beareth not the sword in vain: for he is the minister of God, a revenger to execute wrath upon him that doeth evil" (Rom. 13:4).*

Prayer: Lord Jesus Christ, Son of God, have mercy on us.[1] Our land needs your mercy and love in these last days when perilous times are upon us.[2] The hearts of people are failing them for fear.[3] I thank you that those of us who know you do not need to fear because we know you are coming in great power and glory.[4]

Father, your perfect love casts out all fear.[5] I rejoice in the knowledge that you have replaced a spirit of fear in my life with your power, love and a sound mind.[6] May the leaders and law enforcement officials of our land discover your love, walk in its security and respond to people in your love, authority and power.

God, I thank you that you so loved the world that you sent your only begotten Son so that whoever would believe in Him would have eternal life.[7] I pray for a revival in our land that would lead millions to believe in Jesus. Ultimately, I realize, this is the answer; as you change the hearts of men, the statistics related to crime and violence will decrease. Send a heaven-borne revival to America, Father; I ask for this in the name of Jesus.[8]

The stresses and strains that are faced daily by the police and their families are incomparable. I beseech you in behalf of each law enforcement official that you would reveal your love to each one, helping him or her to realize that in you there is redemption, even the forgiveness of sins.[9] Impart wisdom to these men and women as they face the challenges of each day. Protect them and keep them from the evil one.[10]

Restore a respect for authority among our people in this crucial hour. Affirm your power to law enforcement officials and remind each one of his or her need to be in subjection to you.[11] Help me and my fellow citizens always to pray for and respect these men and women who risk their lives for us.[12]

Lord, open the eyes of our people and the governing authorities to the realization that every soul should be subject unto your higher power because there is no power except that which you give. Help police officers to know that their powers are ordained of you, and to rest in the fact that those who resist your power when it is properly administered through law enforcement agents are resisting the ordinance you have established to protect our people. Because this is true, we never need to fear their power unless we join the ranks of the unruly and disobedient. Help Americans to remember that love never works ill toward their neighbors and that love is the fulfillment of your law, Lord.[13]

References: (1)Matthew 9:27; (2)2 Timothy 3:1; (3)Luke 21:26; (4)Luke 21:27; (5)1 John 4:18; (6)2 Timothy 1:7; (7)John 3:16; (8)John 16:23-24; (9)Ephesians 1:7; (10)2 Thessalonians 3:3; (11)Romans 13:1; (12)1 Timothy 2:1-3; (13)Romans 13:2-10.

Lawlessness and Crime

Key Thought: The law provides a rudder for the ship of state.

Key Scripture: *"Knowing this, that the law is not made for a righteous man, but for the lawless and disobedient, for the ungodly and for sinners, for unholy and profane, for murderers of fathers and murderers of mothers, for manslayers, For whoremongers, for them that defile themselves with mankind, for menstealers, for liars, for perjured persons, and if there be any other thing that is contrary to sound doctrine"* (1 Tim. 1:9-10).

Prayer: Thank you, Father, for the Constitution of the United States and for all the laws of our land, many of which have their origin in the principles of your blessed Word. Restore a spirit of obedience to and respect for the laws of our land.

Lord God, so many are walking according to the course of this world, according to the prince of the power of the air who leads people into all forms of disobedience.[1] Show the exceeding riches of your grace to the lawless and disobedient in our society so that the waves of crime and violence will be permanently eradicated.[2]

Lord, I know all too well how you brought me to life and obedience when I was dead in my sins, and I now ask you to convict the criminals, members of crime syndicates, gangs, thieves, murderers, extortionists, liars, fornicators and all who are engaged in lawlessness to recognize their sins and to repent of their evil acts.[3] I thank you, Father, that it is your goodness that leads us to repentance.[4]

Please grant the spirit of repentance to the lawless and disobedient in America who walk in darkness.[5] Reveal to them the truth that even though all have sinned and fallen short of your glory,[6] you have commended your love toward us in that while we were yet sinners, you died for us, precious Lord.[7] Father, speak to the hearts of the lawless and disobedient, convicting them of their sins and leading them to salvation through faith in Jesus Christ.[8] I praise you that your free gift to all who come to you in faith and repentance is eternal life.[9]

Through faith in your Word, Lord, I come against the stronghold of lawlessness that enshrouds our society. I cast down imaginations and every high thing that exalts itself against the knowledge of God and I bring into captivity every thought to the obedience of Christ.[10]

In light of all the disobedience around me, Lord, I choose to mortify my members which are upon the earth. I die to sin and disobedience in my life. Warn Americans of your wrath which will come upon the children of disobedience.[11]

Open the eyes of my fellow-citizens so that they will be able to see that the supreme law — the law on which all laws are based — is to love you with all our hearts, minds and souls and to love our neighbors as ourselves.[12]

References: *(1)Ephesians 2:2; (2)Ephesians 2:7; (3)Ephesians 2:2-7; (4)Romans 2:4; (5)Acts 11:18; (6)Romans 3:23; (7)Romans 5:18; (8)2 Timothy 2:10; (9)Romans 6:23; (10)2 Corinthians 10:3-5; (11)Colossians 3:5-6; (12)Matthew 22:37-39.*

Marriages

Key Thought: Marriage is not to be entered into lightly or unadvisedly.

Key Scripture: *"For this cause shall a man leave his father and mother, and shall be joined unto his wife, and they two shall be one flesh. This is a great mystery: but I speak concerning Christ and the church. Nevertheless let every one of you in particular so love his wife even as himself; and the wife see that she reverence her husband"* *(Eph. 5:31-33).*

Prayer: Strengthen the marriages of our land, Lord, during this time when the furies of hell have been unleashed against married couples and families. Reveal to husbands and wives the sacredness and importance of marriage. Restore the values of faithfulness, caring and commitment to marriages today.

Lord, I ask you to call our married couples back to yourself. Lead husbands and wives and children in American families today, to salvation and eternal life through Jesus Christ, our Lord.[1]

Teach husbands and wives how to submit themselves to each other in fear of you. Lead wives to submit themselves unto their own husbands as unto you. Show husbands how to love their wives even as you, Lord Jesus, love your bride, the Church.[2]

Father, I thank you that you are calling families back to you. Be a guide and companion to the following couples who face the challenges of a troubled marriage: _____ _____ .
Help them to know your will for them and may these individuals find hope for their hearts and their marriages in you, as they learn to live "each for the other and both for you."

So many couples are being divorced and so many children are being affected. God, I know you hate divorce because you are the Husband of your Church and you are zealous to guard the commitment you have to your people. Give the husbands of our land this same protective zeal and commitment.

When Joshua affirmed, "As for me and my house, we will serve the Lord," I am sure that he was setting a godly example for all of us to follow.[3] Raise up many Joshuas in our land today and enable the world to see the beauty and value of a home where you are the Lord.

Help parents to see that there is no more important ministry than their charge to raise their children in your nurture and admonition.[4] It is through this kind of wisdom that a home is built and by understanding it is established.[5] May each husband and wife be able to look upon the other in the same way you look upon them. As Solomon pointed out, you look upon your beloved as being fair, with no blemishes.[6] Let us behold our spouses with the eyes of love.

Let those who are contemplating marriage recognize your purpose and your values as they plan for their weddings. Instill in the clergypeople of our land a strong desire to guide engaged couples into godly marriages.

Rekindle dying embers of love in the hearts of marriage partners who are disenchanted and discouraged. Father, send your Word and heal them.[7] Lead wives to remember that they can help their husbands through prayer and righteous living.[8] Help husbands to comprehend that they have the same responsibility toward their wives and to remember that a prudent wife is from you.[9] Teach married couples how to forbear with one another in your love,[10] to be tender-hearted and forgiving to each other at all times.[11]

I ask, O heavenly Father, that you would impart to all of us a renewed sense of hope and purpose for the American family. Help us to catch a glimpse of your vision for the American home. In so doing, we will be able to prepare for generations to come so that they might know your blessing and your ways — even the children which are yet to be born. May they, likewise, declare your truths to their children so that all succeeding generations will be able to set their hope in you.[12]

References: *(1)Romans 6:23; (2)Ephesians 5:21-25; (3)Joshua 24:15; (4)Ephesians 6:4; (5)Proverbs 24:3; (6)Song of Solomon 5; (7)Psalms 107:20; (8)1 Peter 3:1,2; (9)Proverbs 19:14; (10)Ephesians 4:2; (11)Ephesians 4:32; (12)Psalms 78:6-7.*

The Media

Key Thought: The media's influence in our culture is far-reaching.

Key Scripture: *"How beautiful upon the mountains are the feet of him that bringeth good tidings, that publisheth peace; that bringeth good tidings of good, that publisheth salvation; that saith unto Zion, Thy God reigneth!" (Isa. 52:7).*

Prayer: Heavenly Father, for many years we've watched the gradual desensitization of our society as a result of some media that have become saturated with sexual immorality, profanity, violence and rebellion in both print and broadcast realms. I ask you to convict the hearts of the producers and other media representatives of their need to be both responsible and caring with regard to programing and publishing. I ask you, Lord, to convict them in their own consciences.[1]

Guard the minds of children, young people and impressionable adults from the mental manipulation that often occurs through television, radio, motion pictures, music and other sources. Help me, and all who know your name, to be not conformed to this world, but rather to be transformed by the renewing of our minds that we may be able to prove what is your good and perfect and acceptable will.[2]

Lord, you are the Rock. Your work is perfect. All your ways are judgment. You are a God of truth and you are without iniquity — you are completely just and right. Many of the people of your creation have corrupted themselves; they have become a perverse and crooked generation. Help the people of our nation to remember the days of old, to acknowledge you as their Creator and Establisher, to appreciate all you have done for us.[3]

Let there be a return to wholesome programing in the media. May motion pictures and other dramatic forms present values that are consistent with the Judeo-Christian ethic upon which our nation was founded. Return our national focus to whatsoever things are just, pure, of good report, true, lovely and righteous for we know that if there be any virtue or praise, these are the things that must take priority in our national consciousness.[4]

Inspire our leaders to bring our national priorities in line with yours, O Lord. Move on their hearts to seek counsel from your mouth[5] and to incline their ears to your wisdom[6] and their hearts to the understanding you alone can give.[7] Break through to media representatives and advertisers and convince them of their need to follow suit and of their need for responsibility and accountability to you and to this nation.

Lord God, I beseech you to pour out your Spirit upon all the people of our nation. Convict them of sin. Convince them of their need for your righteousness. Bring them unto repentance,[8] saving faith in Jesus Christ[9] and fill them with your Holy Spirit.[10] Let them receive power when the Holy Spirit comes upon them and be witnesses for Jesus Christ in their home towns, in all of America and to the ends of the earth.[11] Use the media of our nation to help bring this to pass.

References: (1)John 8:9; (2)Romans 12:2; (3)Deuteronomy 32:4-7; (4)Philippians 4:8; (5)Joshua 9:14; (6)Proverbs 2:2,6; (7)Psalms 119:34; (8)Acts 3:19; (9)John 3:16; (10)Acts 2:38; (11)Acts 1:8.

Medical Professionals

Key Thought: All healing comes from God.

Key Scripture: *"He was wounded for our transgressions, he was bruised for our iniquities: the chastisement of our peace was upon him; and with his stripes we are healed"* *(Isa. 53:5).*

Prayer: Lord, I thank you that you are the Great Physician, the healer of our souls and bodies. You are the One who heals us.[1] You restore my soul and you lead me in the paths of righteousness for your name's sake.[2] Be with our doctors, nurses, technicians, therapists and other medical professionals. Help them to acknowledge their utter dependence on you[3] and to humble themselves under your mighty hand.[4]

You have loved me with an everlasting love, and with your lovingkindness you have drawn me to yourself.[5] Draw the medical professionals and their patients to yourself, and make them aware of your everlasting lovingkindness, Father.[6]

Impart your precious wisdom to all those who have to make important decisions about health care — to the families of the sick, to the physicians and all involved in the important work of healing. Help them to know that fearing you, the Mighty God, is the beginning of that wisdom.[7] You took our infirmities and you bore our sicknesses.[8] You are interested in the health and healing of people.[9] You are full of love and compassion.[10]

Your promise to your people, Father, is that you desire to take all sickness away from them.[11] Lead our medical professionals to incline their ears unto wisdom and apply their hearts unto understanding. May they seek wisdom as silver and search for it as for hidden treasures. Then shall they understand the right kind of fear with which to approach you and their important work of healing. Then shall they find the knowledge of God. Keep them, Father, in that blessed understanding.[12]

Lord, I thank you for the cures, vaccines and inoculations that have been discovered for so many diseases. Bless and guide all those who are involved in medical research. Lead them to the cures for the diseases that affect our population — cancer, multiple sclerosis, AIDS, heart disease and other afflictions.

Help doctors and nurses to see the power of prayer; reveal that power to them, Father. Even as Jesus continued all night in prayer, may they learn to seek your face as they contemplate the important responsibilities of their lives.[13]

Father, show America how to reduce the cost of health care through preventive medicine and good health practices. Help our medical professionals to understand the relationship that sometimes exists between unrighteousness and sickness, that the work of healing often involves forgiveness and faith has great power to effect healing in people's lives. Lord, you have declared that the prayer of faith shall save the sick, and you shall raise him up. Bring forth many healings in our land in response to the prayers of your people. [14]

References: (1)Exodus 15:26; (2)Psalms 23:3; (3)John 15:5; (4)1 Peter 5:6; (5)Jeremiah 31:3; (6)Psalms 36:7; (7)Psalms 111:10; (8)Matthew 8:17; (9)Psalms 103:3; (10)Psalms 86:15; (11)Deuteronomy 7:15; (12)Proverbs 2:2-11; (13)Luke 6:12; (14)James 5:15-16.

Mental Health

Key Thought: God's peace guards your heart and mind.

Key Scripture: *"Fear thou not; for I am with thee: be not dismayed; for I am thy God: I will strengthen thee; yea, I will help thee; yea, I will uphold thee with the right hand of my righteousness"* (Isa. 41:10).

Prayer: Heavenly Father, I thank you that you have not given us a spirit of fear, but of power, love and a sound mind.[1] I pray for the people of our land who suffer from fear and from other mental afflictions; let them take hold of your strength, precious Lord, so that they would be able to make peace with you.[2] Dear Lord, it is my privilege right now to lift up to you the following individual(s) who is/are suffering from mental illness:_____

_____ . Be a very present help to them,[3] and help them appropriate your peace which passes all understanding.[4] It is your wonderful peace, Lord Jesus Christ, that keeps our hearts and minds in tact.

Be with all the pastors, doctors, counselors, nurses, social workers and others who care for those who suffer from mental illness. Fill them with compassion, empathy, wisdom and power, Lord, by leading them to find your strength that will enable them to accomplish your purposes. In dealing with those who suffer from mental afflictions, help all of us in America to have patience and love for them.[5]

Father, send your ministers to those afflicted with mental illness. Empower these ministers with the anointing of your Spirit to preach the gospel as needed, to heal the broken-hearted and to set the sick free from their captivity.[6] Lord, restore health to them and heal them of all their wounds.[7]

Lord, you always redeem the souls of your servants, and no one who trusts in you shall ever be desolate.[8] By fearing you, any person can have strong confidence and a place of refuge.[9] Fill the mental hospitals of our land with your presence and destroy the strongholds of the enemy within them.[10] Lead all workers and patients in mental hospitals to a saving knowledge of your love through faith in Jesus Christ.[11]

I thank you, Father, that you satisfy the hungry soul and fill it with goodness. Those who sit in darkness and in the shadow of death can cry to you in their trouble and you will save them out of their distress. Lord, break their bands asunder. Set them free.[12] In your mighty name, I come against the destroyer who seeks to devour the souls and bodies of our people.[13] Rebuke him, Lord, and restore hope to those who are cast down.[14]

God, you are not the author of confusion.[15] Your goal is to set the captives free.[16] When we call unto you, you always answer. I ask you to satisfy the afflicted soul; let your light rise in his or her obscurity; let the darkness of their souls become as the noonday.[17]

Teach all those who are afflicted mentally that their faith will make them whole, to fear not, but only believe so that they would experience the wholeness you want them to have.[18]

Thank you, heavenly Father, for answering my prayer which is offered to you in the incomparable name of Jesus.

References: (1)2 Timothy 1:7; (2)Isaiah 27:5; (3)Psalms 46:1; (4)Philippians 4:7; (5)James 1:4; (6)Luke 4:18; (7)Jeremiah 30:17; (8)Psalms 34:22; (9)Proverbs 14:26; (10)2 Corinthians 10:4-5; (11)Philippians 3:9; (12)Psalms 107:9-15; (13)1 Peter 5:8; (14)Psalms 42:11; (15)1 Corinthians 14:33; (16)Luke 4:18; (17)Isaiah 58:7-11; (18)Luke 8:48,50.

Natural Disasters

Key Thought: Jesus is a rock in a weary land, a shelter in the time of storm.

Key Scripture: *"And every one that heareth these sayings of mine, and doeth them not, shall be likened unto a foolish man, which built his house upon the sand: And the rain descended, and the floods came, and the winds blew, and beat upon that house; and it fell: and great was the fall of it"* *(Matt. 7:26-27).*

Prayer: Heavenly Father, help America to be like the wise man who built his house upon the rock so that when the rains and storms unleash their fury within our borders, our people will be able to stand without fear.[1] How I thank you and praise you that we have no reason to fear when natural disasters assail because we are of more value to you than many sparrows — more valuable than we can possibly imagine.[2] Bring revival to America so that all our citizens will know how much you love them.[3]

Keep our people from fear when they are forced to endure earthquakes, floods, fires, tornadoes, hurricanes, blizzards, volcanoes, storms and other natural disasters. Protect our people and help them to know that you will be with them always, even unto the end of the world,[4] if they will acknowledge Jesus Christ as their Lord.[5]

Help us to discern your still, small voice in the midst of natural disasters as Elijah did when the wind rent the mountains and broke the rocks in pieces before you. Then an earthquake came, followed by a fire, but you were not in the earthquake and you were not in the fire.[6] Lord, lead men and women of our nation to you in the aftermath of natural disasters.

Lord, I thank you that those who know you have no reason to fear natural disasters, for your Word assures us that you are our refuge and strength, a very present help in trouble. Therefore, we will not fear, though the earth be removed, and though the mountains be carried into the midst of the sea. We will not fear though the waters roar and be troubled and though the mountains shake with the swelling thereof. You are in the midst of your people. We shall not be moved because you are with us.[7]

I lift up to you all those who have been victims of natural disasters, Lord. Many have lost their loved ones, their homes, their personal possessions. Comfort those who mourn,[8] sustain all those who cast their burdens upon you.[9] Help those with financial losses. Supply all of their needs according to your riches in glory by Christ Jesus.[10]

References: *(1)Matthew 7:24-25; (2)Matthew 10:31; (3)Romans 5:8; (4)Matthew 28:20; (5)Colossians 2:6; (6)1 Kings 19:11-12; (7)Psalms 46:1-7; (8)Matthew 5:4; (9)Psalms 55:22; (10)Philippians 4:19.*

Peace and Safety

Key Thought: "There is a place of quiet rest near to the heart of God."

Key Scripture: *"The eternal God is thy refuge, and underneath are the everlasting arms: and he shall thrust out the enemy from before thee" (Deut. 33:27).*

Prayer: Dear heavenly Father, our sovereign Lord, how I thank you that you are our refuge and strength, a very present help in trouble.[1] Reveal this truth to the leaders and citizens of our country. Help all of us to know that there is no need to fear even though the earth be removed and though the mountains be carried into the midst of the sea because you are with us.[2] Lead the people of our land to trust in you at all times because you are our rock and our salvation. You are our defense — our refuge, our place of peace and safety.[3]

You are a strength to the poor, a strength to the needy in his distress, a refuge from the storm, a shadow from the heat.[4] Oh, that men would learn to praise you for your goodness to us.[5]

Teach our citizens not to oppress one another. Help us all to learn to fear you with a holy fear for you are our Lord and our God. Teach us to do your statutes, Lord, and to observe your judgments. By so doing, we all need to realize, we shall be able to dwell in the land in safety, and the land shall yield its fruit and we will be able to eat our fill.[6]

Help our leaders always to remember that even though we make preparations against the day of battle, safety is of you.[7] Though the arm of flesh will fail us, you will take us up.[8]Show the truth to our president that no king is saved by the multitude of a host, and a mighty man is not saved by much strength.[9] We are saved only by you.

Lord, so many people live without regard to your truth. Reveal to our citizens that your day will come as a thief in the night, when we least expect it. When people will be saying, "Peace and safety," then sudden destruction will come. Help all of us who know you, Lord Jesus, to truly be the children of light. Help us not to sleep or to be idle, but teach us to watch and be sober. Help us to lead many into a saving knowledge of your love and grace[10] through receiving Jesus as their Lord.[11]

Great peace have they which love your law, Lord. Nothing shall offend them.[12] Lead the people of our country to love your law and to find their peace and safety in you. Glory to you in the highest, and on earth, impart your peace and your goodwill toward men.[13]

References: (1)Psalms 46:1; (2)Psalms 46:2-7; (3)Psalms 62:6-8; (4)Isaiah 25:4; (5)Psalms 107:8; (6)Leviticus 25:17-19; (7)Proverbs 21:31; (8)Job 26:2; (9)Psalms 33:16; (10)1 Thessalonians 5:2-8; (11)1 Thessalonians 5:9; (12)Psalms 119:165; (13)Luke 2:14.

Pornography

Key Thought: "The penalty of sin is that gradually you get used to it and do not know that it is sin" (Oswald Chambers).

Key Scripture: *"Finally, brethren, whatsoever things are true, whatsoever things are honest, whatsoever things are just, whatsoever things are pure, whatsoever things are lovely, whatsoever things are of good report; if there be any virtue, and if there be any praise, think on these things" (Phil. 4:8).*

Prayer: O Holy One of Israel, God of goodness, purity and light, I beseech you to restore purity and holiness to our land. Gradually, our culture is becoming desensitized to the point that even your people, the very elect, are being deceived by the lures of pornography and the lust of the eyes.[1] In your name, Lord, I raise the standard of holiness over our land, and I implore you to remove the blindness of our people who are falling prey to the pride of life, the lust of the flesh and the lust of the eyes.[2]

Through television, motion pictures and magazines — and through lascivious performances on stage — the minds of many are being darkened.[3] Restore to our nation a sense of decency, honor, shame and purity that has been lost to us in recent years.

Lord, I beseech you to remind your people that we are to have no fellowship with the unfruitful works of darkness (such as pornography in its various forms), but rather it is our responsibility to reprove and expose them. Keep it in the forefront of our minds, Lord, that it is a shame to speak of those things that are done in secret.[4]

How I praise you, Father, that your grace that brings salvation has appeared unto all men, teaching us that denying ungodliness and worldly lusts, we should live soberly, righteously and godly in this present world — looking for that blessed hope and your glorious appearing.[5]

Teach our people that if they fail to hearken to your voice, they remain in danger of being given up unto their own hearts' lusts[6] and unto a reprobate mind.[7]

I pray especially for _____ _____ who is/are addicted to pornography. Set him/her free from the snares of the devil, Father. I come against the following purveyors of pornography in our community, Lord: _____ _____ . Help these businesspeople to see that they are selling products that are extremely harmful to our young people, our women and our men.

Bring revival to our land. Convict the consciences of pornographers who seem not to care about how they are destroying the values of our country, disrupting families, leading many into sins of passion, sexual immorality and violence.[8] Open their eyes, Lord. Turn them from darkness to light, and from the power and authority of Satan unto God, so that they will be saved.[9]

In the mighty name of Jesus,[10] God, I ask you for revival in America. Revival so great that the money spent on pornography "dries up" and the porno business can't keep operating. Where sin abounds, your grace much more abounds.[11] All things are possible with you, O God.[12]

References: *(1)Matthew 24:24; (2)1 John 2:15; (3)Romans 1:21; (4)Ephesians 5:11-12; (5)Titus 2:11-12; (6)Psalms 81:11-12; (7)Romans 1:28; (8)John 8:9; (9)Acts 26:18; (10)John 16:23-24; (11)Romans 5:20; (12)Matthew 19:26.*

The Poor

Key Thought: Only what we give away do we keep for all eternity.

Key Scripture: *"Hearken, my beloved brethren, Hath not God chosen the poor of this world rich in faith, and heirs of the kingdom which he hath promised to them that love him? But ye have despised the poor. . . . If ye fulfill the royal law according to the scripture, Thou shalt love thy neighbor as thyself, ye do well: But if ye have respect to persons, ye commit sin, and are convinced of the law as transgressors"* *(James 2:5-8).*

Prayer: Heavenly Father, your Word points out that we will always have the poor with us,[1] and you showed us one important way to minister to them: by preaching the gospel to the poor.[2] I thank you, Master, that ultimately the gospel is the answer to poverty and so many other ills within our land.

Many people in the world, and in our own country, go to bed hungry each night and wake up hungry each morning. I pray for them, Lord, and I ask you to minister to their deepest needs — both physically and spiritually. Help me to respond to this need by feeding the hungry, by inviting the poor to eat with me. You have said that by doing so I would be blessed.[3] Thank you, Lord.

Your amazing grace, Lord Jesus, bestows repentance upon my heart, for I realize that it is your goodness that leads me to acknowledge my wrong attitudes toward the poor and the tendency toward materialism that exists in my own heart.[4] I repent of being judgmental and of the materialism that has often motivated me.

Keep us, as a nation and as individuals, from hardening our hearts and shutting our hands to the poor. You have commanded us to open our hands wide unto the poor and to give them enough so that their needs will be met.[5] Continue to prosper America, Lord, so we will be able to demonstrate your compassion and concern for the poor. Thank you for your promise that he who has pity on the poor lends to you, O Lord, and you will bless him.[6]

Hear the cry of the poor, and save them out of all their troubles.[7] You are so gracious, Father, to the poor and to all who consider their needs. To those who minister to the poor you have promised to preserve them and keep them alive, to bless them upon the earth and to deliver them from their enemies.[8] Dear Father, protect the missionaries, social workers, medical professionals and others who minister to the poor in our country and around the world. Call many to this important work.

O God, our almighty and sovereign Lord, I beseech you to defend the poor and fatherless. Do justice to the afflicted and needy. Deliver them and remove them from the hand of wicked oppressors who would take advantage of their poverty.[9]

How I praise you, Father, for your promise in behalf of the poor. When the poor and needy seek water, and their tongues fail for thirst, you will hear their cries and you will not forsake them. You will open rivers in high places, and fountains in the midst of the valleys. You will make the wilderness a pool of water and you will turn the dry land into springs of water. You, the Holy One of Israel, will accomplish this, and the people of our nation will rejoice in you.[10]

References: (1)John 12:8; (2)Luke 4:18; (3)Luke 14:14; (4)Romans 2:4; (5)Deuteronomy 15:6-8; (6)Proverbs 19:17; (7)Psalms 34:6; (8)Psalms 41:1-2; (9)Psalms 82:3-5; (10)Isaiah 41:17-20.

The President of the United States

Key Thought: No leader can go forward any faster than the people will follow.

Key Scripture: *"I exhort therefore, that, first of all, supplications, prayers, intercessions, and giving of thanks, be made for all men; For kings, and for all that are in authority; that we may lead a quiet and peaceable life in all godliness and honesty"* (1 Tim. 2:1-2).

Prayer: Heavenly Father, I come before you in the mighty name of Jesus Christ. Thank you, Father, for your servant, _____, the President of the United States of America. It is comforting and reassuring to know that his heart is in your hands and, like the rivers of water, you turn it in whatever directions you choose.[1]

Lord, I beseech you to turn our president's heart in the direction of all your ways, because your way is perfect, your Word is tried, and you are a buckler to all those who trust in you.[2]

Father, I pray for the president that if he does not have a personal relationship with Jesus Christ, that he would be converted,[3] receive Jesus as his Lord[4] and be born again by your Spirit.[5]

I pray, if the president is saved, that you would draw him ever closer to you and work in him by your Spirit to will and to do your good pleasure.[6] I ask that as he has therefore received Christ Jesus the Lord, that he would walk in Him; rooted and built up in Him, established in the faith as he has been taught, and abound therein with thanksgiving.[7]

Grant him a spirit of wisdom and revelation in the knowledge of you, the eyes of his understanding being enlightened that he may know the hope of your calling and what is the riches of the glory of your inheritance in the saints and what is the exceeding greatness of your power to him who believes.[8]

I ask that you strengthen him with might by your Spirit in the inner man: that Christ may dwell in his heart through faith; that he being rooted and grounded in love may comprehend with all saints what is the breadth, length, depth and height, and know the love of Christ, which surpasses knowledge and be filled with all of your fullness, O God.[9]

Father, let the seeds of your Word that have been sown in his heart find good ground and spring up in a fruitful harvest of righteousness, godliness and salvation.[10]

Grant unto him the wisdom that is from above — true wisdom that is first pure, then peaceable, gentle, and easy to be entreated, full of good fruits, without partiality, and without hypocrisy.[11]

Establish him in your wisdom and your righteousness. Let your Word be a lamp unto his feet and a light unto his path.[12] He who rules over men must be just, ruling in the fear of God.[13] Father, bless our president with wisdom and justice that come from reverently fearing you. Remind him that the fear of the Lord is the beginning of knowledge,[14] and that whosoever hearkens unto you shall dwell safely, and shall be quiet from fear of evil.[15]

Provide the president with the power and skills he needs to be a peacemaker in his relationships with other leaders, the Congress of the United States and all other people. Lord Jesus, you showed us the way in peace as in all other areas, by declaring, "Blessed are the peacemakers: for they shall be called the children of God." [16] May he be so filled with peace and the ways of peace that others will see him as your child and desire to follow his example.

Father, protect our president from all evil as he deals with the issues of an evil and adulterous generation. [17] By his submission to you may many others realize the importance of submission to the governing authorities, for we realize that there is no authority but yours, and the authorities that be are ordained by you. [18]

Give our president the courage, [19] wisdom, knowledge, discretion and understanding to disentangle himself from any unholy alliances formed in the political process. [20] Let all such alliances be cut off and their effects destroyed. [21] Let all righteous alliances flourish and prosper for the blessing of the president and of America. [22]

Bless the president and his family with all spiritual blessings in heavenly places in Christ. Thank you for choosing him before the foundation of the world. [23] Bless his vice president, _____

_____ , and his family with your spiritual graces and gifts.

Teach your people, Lord, to pray for our leaders so that we may lead a quiet and peaceable life in all godliness and honesty, [24] and help us to be thankful for them. Give us a full realization of the importance of prayer for our leaders and for our nation because this is a key to revival and change in our land. Remind us of your Word which says that if your people, which are called by your name, will humble themselves, and pray, and seek your face, and turn from their wicked ways, then you will hear from heaven, and forgive our sin and heal our land.[25]

Fill the White House with the light of your presence, Lord. You give salvation unto kings,[26] and you deliver your people from the sword. Lead our president, his family and the citizens of our country to become the light of the world, a city set upon a hill that cannot be hid.[27]

For our president and his family, I ask that you cover them with your feathers and under your wings may they learn to trust. May your truth be their shield and buckler. Let no evil befall them and give your angels charge over them to keep them in all their ways.[28]

Draw the president to you, Father, and fill his heart with your Spirit and your love that he might set his love on you. Deliver him and set him on high because he knows your name. And as he calls upon you, give him the answers he needs in all his decision-making. Let him know that you will be with him in the time of trouble. Satisfy him with long life and show him your salvation.[29]

References: (1)Proverbs 21:1; (2)Psalms 18:30; (3)Acts 3:19; (4)Romans 10:9-10; (5)John 3:5-7; (6)Philippians 2:13; (7)Colossians 2:6-7 (8)Ephesians 1:17-19; (9)Ephesians 3:16-19; (10)Luke 8:11-15; (11)James 3:17; (12)Psalms 119:105; (13)2 Samuel 23:3; (14)Proverbs 1:7; (15)Proverbs 1:33; (16)Matthew 5:9; (17)Matthew 12:39; (18)Romans 13:1; (19)Joshua 1:7; (20)Proverbs 2:10-15; (21)Psalms 10:15; (22)Psalms 72:7; (23)Ephesians 1:4; (24)1 Timothy 2:1-3; (25)2 Chronicles 7:14; (26)Psalms 144:10; (27)Matthew 5:14; (28)Psalms 91:4,10-11; (29)Psalms 91:14-16.

Prosperity

Key Thought: God owns the wealth in every mine.

Key Scripture: *"If ye walk in my statutes, and keep my commandments, and do them;. Then I will give you rain in due season, and the land shall yield her increase, and the trees of the field shall yield their fruit" (Lev. 26:3-4).*

Prayer: Lord God, how I praise you for the ways in which you have blessed and kept our land. Continue to make your face shine upon our nation, I pray, and be gracious unto us.[1] Give rain to our land, bless us with your prosperity. I thank you for giving this great land to us.[2] Help us to be good stewards of all you have given us.

Bring to the awareness of the American people how you prosper those who invite you to be with them.[3] Lead our people to acquaint themselves with you so that they may live in peace and experience your goodness and your graciousness.[4] Show this nation that if people will obey and serve you, they shall be able to spend their days in prosperity and their years in pleasures.[5] Let the righteous people in our nation flourish like the palm tree; let us grow like the cedars of Lebanon.[6] In the day of prosperity we are joyful, but help us to remember your joy in the day of adversity as well.[7]

Restore health and life where barrenness has come to our land, Father. Thank you for your promise that the parched ground shall become a pool and the thirsty land springs of water.[8] Bring to your people all the good that you have promised.[9] This is the day which you have made; we will rejoice and be glad in it. Save now, I beseech you, O Lord; send prosperity to our land now.[10]

God, I thank you for the certain knowledge that you will prosper your people because you love us,[11] and those who love you will always prosper.[12] Lead the people of our country to remember you, O Lord our God, and to be ever mindful that it is you who gives the power for a nation or an individual to obtain wealth, to establish your covenant[13] and to spread the gospel of salvation through faith in Jesus Christ.[14] All that is in the heaven and in the earth is yours, dear Father. Riches and honor come from you.[15] Indeed, all things come from your hands.[16]

Lead our nation to trust you, Lord, instead of placing its trust in riches,[17] for riches will not profit us at all in the day of wrath,[18] and he that trusts in his riches will fall.[19]

Restore unto our people the value of hard work and personal responsibility, for we know that he who gathers by hard labor shall increase.[20] May we never forget that the silver and the gold are yours, gracious Father.[21]

References: (1)Numbers 6:25; (2)1 Kings 8:36; (3)2 Kings 18:7; (4)Job 22:21; (5)Job 36:11; (6)Psalms 92:12; (7)Ecclesiastes 7:14; (8)Isaiah 35:7; (9)Jeremiah 32:42; (10)Psalms 118:24-25; (11)Nehemiah 2:20; (12)Psalms 122:6; (13)Deuteronomy 8:18; (14)2 Timothy 2:10; (15)1 Chronicles 29:11-12; (16)1 Chronicles 29:14; (17)Proverbs 11:28; (18)Proverbs 11:4; (19)Proverbs 11:28; (20)Proverbs 13:11; (21)Haggai 2:8.

Protection From Disease

Key Thought: God wants His people to walk in health.

Key Scripture: *"Thou shalt not be afraid for the terror by night; nor for the arrow that flieth by day; Nor for the pestilence that walketh in darkness; nor for the destruction that wasteth at noonday. A thousand shall fall at thy side, and ten thousand at thy right hand; but it shall not come nigh thee.... Because thou hast made the Lord, which is my refuge, even the most High, thy habitation; There shall no evil befall thee, neither shall any plague come nigh thy dwelling"* (Ps. 91:5-10).

Prayer: It is a good thing to give thanks unto you, O Lord, and to sing praises unto your name, O most High. Help me to show forth your lovingkindness in the morning, and your faithfulness every night.[1] Thank you for your promise to give your angels charge over me, to keep me in all your ways, and thank you for setting your love upon me and my family.[2]

In a day, Father, when so many forms of disease and pestilence are reappearing in our nation and the world, and previously unknown viruses and illnesses are affecting so many, lead the people of our country to realize that you are the Great Physician of our souls and bodies and that you are able to deliver us from sickness and to protect us from harm.[3]

Lord, send a heaven-born revival to our land[4] so that multitudes[5] will come to know Jesus as their personal Savior and Lord.[6] Then they will be able to recognize Him as the Balm in Gilead,[7] the Lord who heals His people.[8] Then we will have no reason to fear because all of our faith and trust will be in Him.[9]

So many sicknesses that are prevalent in the world today stem from behaviors you have warned us against. Thank you for loving us so much that you have given us these warnings and for admonishing us to flee immorality.[10]

We acknowledge, O Lord, our wickedness, and the iniquity of our fathers: for we have sinned against you. Do not abhor us; for thy name's sake, do not disgrace the throne of your glory. We beseech you not to break your covenant with us, your people, and your covenant with our nation. So many cry, "Why have you smitten us, and there is no healing for us?" Therefore, we will wait upon you because you are our Deliverer.[11]

Father, remind me and my fellow Americans to attend to your words, to keep them before our eyes and in the midst of our hearts. For they are life to those who find them and health to all their flesh.[12]

O God, I pray that the people of America will make you, the Most High, their Lord, their refuge and their habitation. For then no evil shall befall them and no plague shall come near their dwellings. And you shall give your angels charge over them, to keep them in all their ways.[13]

Thank you, Father, for the water of life. It is clear as crystal and it proceeds out of your throne. Thank you also for the Tree of Life, my precious Savior Jesus Christ.

Your Word declares that the leaves of the tree are for the healing of the nations, that there shall be no more curses for your Kingdom will rule forever. Hasten that day, Lord. May the leaves of the Tree of Life bring healing to our nation. May our people see your face and serve you.[14]

References: *(1)Psalms 92:1-2; (2)Psalms 91:11-14; (3)1 Samuel 26:24; (4)Psalms 85:6; (5)Matthew 4:25; (6)Romans 10:8-9; (7)Jeremiah 8:22; (8)Exodus 15:26; (9)Psalms 34:4; (10)2 Timothy 2:22; (11)Jeremiah 14:19-22; (12)Proverbs 4:20-22; (13)Psalms 91:9-11; (14)Revelation 22:1-4.*

Racism

Key Thought: A prejudice knows no logic.

Key Scripture: *"Then Peter opened his mouth, and said, Of a truth I perceive that God is no respecter of persons: But in every nation he that feareth him, and worketh righteousness, is accepted with him" (Acts 10:34-35).*

Prayer: God, I thank you that you are not a respecter of persons,[1] and that while people often look on the outward appearances of people, you judge people by their hearts. I thank you, Lord, that you don't see as man sees,[2] and I thank you that you want us to follow you in all things and you have given us your Spirit to enable us to do so. I want to follow you, Master.

Help me never to judge people according to their color, their race, their nationality, their economic class or any other superficial standard. You have commanded us not to judge so that we will not be judged. Lord, I realize the truth of your Word that proclaims that we will be judged with the same judgment we render and we will be measured by the same standard we use to measure others.[3] I repent of all prejudice that I have held and expressed toward others because they differ from me in the color of their skin, their nationality, their economic class or their race.

Father, I repent on behalf of the United States of America for our attitudes of racism and prejudice. I repent also for the acts of evil and wickedness which we have done to one another for far too long. We have sinned;[4] have mercy on us.[5]

Call our nation to repentance before you and grant our people godly sorrow that will work true repentance in our hearts to confess our sins of racism and prejudice.[6]

Father, I know that the only true solution to our racism and prejudice is to have our hearts changed[7] through receiving Jesus Christ as our Savior and Lord.[8]

Therefore, Father, I ask you to pour out your grace upon our people and send revival to America.[9] Let racism and prejudice be destroyed in our nation as overwhelming numbers of all races, colors and creeds receive Jesus Christ as their Lord and Savior[10] and thereby have your love shed abroad in their hearts by the Holy Spirit.[11]

Heavenly Father, it is disturbing to see racism in our land. I praise your name and pray that when the enemy comes in like a flood, your Spirit will raise a standard against him.[12]

Tear down the walls that divide our people, Lord. You are able to bring unity out of diversity. Reconcile our citizens to you and to one another.[13]

Empower the people of your Church, Lord, to lead the way in our land by observing your truth and practicing your love without preferring one before another, doing nothing by partiality.[14] Help us to remember at all times that your wisdom is without partiality and without hypocrisy, and that the fruit of righteousness is sown in peace of them who make peace.[15]

Father, all these things I pray in the incomparable name of my Lord Jesus Christ.[16]

References: *(1)Acts 10:34; (2)1 Samuel 16:7; (3)Matthew 7:1-2; (4)Daniel 9:3-5; (5)Psalms 85:7; (6)2 Corinthians 7:10; (7)Ezekiel 36:26; (8)Hebrews 10:22; (9)Titus 2:11; (10)Romans 10:9-10; (11)Romans 5:5; (12)Isaiah 59:19; (13)Ephesians 2:14-16; (14)1 Timothy 5:21; (15)James 3:18; (16)John 16:23.*

Revival in the Land

Key Thought: God loves you!

Key Scripture: *"Jesus saith unto him, I am the way, the truth, and the life: no man cometh unto the Father, but by me"* (John 14:6).

Prayer: Lord, I thank you that you are the God of revival. You desire to impart new life to the redeemed and salvation to the lost. Thank you for sending Jesus, your Son, to save that which was lost.[1] It is not your will for any to perish, but for all to come to a knowledge of your saving grace.[2]

Send revival to America, Lord. Draw men, women and young people to you for you are truly our only hope. Reveal the truth to people everywhere — that they can be saved only by grace, through faith, and that is not of themselves, but it is your gift to them.[3] Thank you for saving me, Lord. Help me to be a witness wherever I go and an intercessor at all times. Teach me how to be joyful always, to pray without ceasing and in everything to give thanks for I know this is your will for me.[4]

Thank you, Lord God, for commending your love toward us in that while we were yet sinners, you sent your Son to die for us.[5] Jesus is the propitiation, the atoning sacrifice, for our sins, and not for ours only, but for the sins of the whole world.[6] Help the people of our nation to see that the wages of sin is death, but your gift to people is eternal life through Jesus Christ, our Lord.[7]

Be relentless, O God. Give the people of our nation no rest until they say yes to you. Bring every person within our borders into a personal encounter with your Spirit[8] and the Gospel of Jesus Christ.[9] Give them grace to repent[10] and receive Jesus as their Lord and Savior.[11]

For our country, Father, I ask that as Jesus was raised up from the dead by your glory, that you would raise up our nation to walk in newness of life.[12] Anoint the ministers and evangelists of our land to proclaim your truth boldly so that many who hear your Word will believe in the same way many did in the early days of your Church when Peter and John went forth in your name.[13]

Neither is there salvation in any other than you, Jesus. There is no other name under heaven given among men whereby we must be saved.[14] Revive us again, O Lord. Show our nation your mercy, and grant us your salvation. Turn us, O God of our salvation, for surely your salvation is nigh them that fear you so that glory may dwell in our land.[15]

I thank you that your hand is not shortened. You still save all who come to you in faith. Your ear is not heavy; you still hear those who cry out to you.[16]

Intervene in the affairs and values of our nation, O Lord, so that many shall fear your name, and behold your glory from the rising of the sun. I know that when the enemy shall come in like a flood, your Spirit will lift up a standard against him. And you, Lord Jesus Christ, our Redeemer, will come to us and unto all that turn from their transgressions.[17] Praise your holy name.

References: *(1)Matthew 18:11; (2)2 Peter 3:9; (3)Ephesians 2:8,9; (4)1 Thessalonians 5:16-18; (5)Romans 5:8; (6)1 John 2:2; (7)Romans 6:23; (8)1 Corinthians 12:3; (9)2 Corinthians 9:13; (10)Romans 2:4; (11)John 1:12 (12)Romans 6:4; (13)Acts 4; (14)Acts 4:12; (15)Psalms 85:4-7,9; (16)Isaiah 59:1-4; (17)Isaiah 59:19-20.*

Righteousness

Key Thought: Righteousness expresses the will of God.

Key Scripture: *"Righteousness exalteth a nation: but sin is a reproach to any people"* *(Prov. 14:34).*

Prayer: Return a spirit of righteousness to the United States of America, Father, for this is what our nation needs — righteous people who put you first in their lives. Lead us all to seek first your righteousness and your kingdom, for in so doing everything else we need will be added unto us.[1]

I pray that all our people will receive the free gift of righteousness that you have promised to all who accept Jesus Christ as their Lord.[2]

Thank you for showing me that all my righteousness is as filthy rags in your sight, O Lord; I am incapable of producing righteousness in my life, but you are my righteousness.[3] Through the blessed life of Abraham you have shown us the important connection between faith and righteousness, Lord, for as Abraham believed in you, you counted it to him for righteousness.[4] Impart your gift of faith to our nation, Father, so that our citizens will learn to walk in righteousness.

Lord, it is not because of our righteousness that you have allowed us to possess this great land, but it is simply because of your good pleasure toward us.[5] Render to each person your righteousness and faithfulness.[6] You show your great mercy to those who walk before you in truth and righteousness and in uprightness of heart.[7] Help Americans everywhere to see this truth, to walk in it and to be thankful for your mercy.

Declare your righteousness to our people, Master.[8] The heavens declare your righteousness and all the people of our land can see your glory.[9] Let them see, Lord; open their eyes.

Lead us in the way of your righteousness, O Lord. Your fruit of righteousness is better than fine gold and you always cause those who love you to inherit your substance. Fill the treasuries of our land, Lord, as our people turn to Christ and to standards of righteous living.[10] Awaken our people to their need for your righteousness so they will learn to sin not. Some don't have the knowledge of you, Father. Awaken them, I pray.[11]

Now, therefore, O our God, hear the prayer of your servant. Hear my supplications and cause your face to shine upon our nation. O my God, incline your ear and hear me. Open your eyes and see the desolation around us, even in a land that knows your name. I do not present my supplications before you because of the righteousness of the United States, but simply because I know your mercies are great. O Lord, hear. O Lord, forgive our people. O Lord, hearken and return us to your righteous standards. Defer not, for your own sake, O my God, for this is a nation that proclaims to trust in you.[12]

References: (1)Matthew 6:33; (2)Romans 5:17; (3)Isaiah 64:6; (4)Genesis 15:6; (5)Deuteronomy 9:6; (6)1 Samuel 26:23; (7)1 Kings 3:6; (8)Psalms 22:31; (9)Psalms 97:6; (10)Proverbs 8:17-21; (11)1 Corinthians 15:34; (12)Daniel 9:18-19.

Role Models

Key Thought: A true hero is a person who cares.

Key Scripture: *"Be thou an example of the believers, in word, in conversation, in charity, in spirit, in faith, in purity. Till I come, give attendance to reading, to exhortation, to doctrine"* (1 Tim. 4:12-13).

Prayer: Dear God, our heavenly Father, thank you for giving us your Son, our Lord Jesus Christ, who gave us an example of how to live so that we should do as He did in all things.[1] Thank you for the power of your example and your Spirit, Lord, who enables us to do all the things you have commanded us to do. Through you, we can do all things.[2] It is certain that without you we can do nothing of any lasting value.[3]

I pray for the young people of our land, many of whom are susceptible to the influences of their role models and heroes. At the same time, Lord, I want to ask you to strengthen and to bless those role models — parents, pastors, teachers, athletes, entertainers, musicians, politicians and others — so that they will be able to be true to the values you have established for godly living[4] and abundant life.[5]

When our role models fall, many people are dismayed and hurt. Therefore, Father, I ask you to lead each role model into a close and personal relationship with you because you are our strength[6] and you are our righteousness.[7] All of our own goodness and righteousness, Father, are as filthy rags in your sight.[8] There is no one who is completely good, not even one.[9] All of us have fallen short of your glory.[10] Teach all of us that ultimately the right life to pattern our own after is Jesus.[11]

At this time, Lord Jesus, I pray for the following individuals who serve as role models in our country today:

_____ . I ask you to deliver them from evil,[12] to teach them your ways,[13] to help them to love your Word. May each one delight to do your will, O Lord.[14] May these role models be able to say with St. Paul, "I have lived in all good conscience before God."[15]

May those role models who do not know you call upon you for salvation so that they will be able to live a godly and righteous life before you and the people of our nation.[16] As a result of their Christian witness,[17] may multitudes of people in the United States and around the world receive Jesus Christ as their Savior and Lord.

Teach me and all your people how to pray effectively for all those who have public influence in our society. Especially, Lord, I know we should be praying for our pastors, youth workers, evangelists, teachers, missionaries and all who are involved in your front-line service. Fill them continually with your Spirit, Lord, so that they will always have the power to serve you and to speak your Word with boldness.[18]

References: (1)John 13:15; (2)Philippians 4:13; (3)John 15:5; (4)Titus 2:12; (5)John 10:10; (6)2 Samuel 22:33; (7)Psalms 4:1; (8)Isaiah 64:6; (9)Psalms 53:3; (10)Romans 3:23; (11)1 John 2:6; (12)Matthew 6:13; (13)Psalms 25:4; (14)Psalms 40:8; (15)Acts 23:1; (16)John 1:12; (17)Acts 1:8; (18)Acts 4:31.

Sexual Immorality

Key Thought: Sexuality is a gift of God.

Key Scripture: *"But ye are a chosen generation, a royal priesthood, an holy nation, a peculiar people; that ye should shew forth the praises of him who hath called you out of darkness into his marvellous light: Dearly beloved, I beseech you as strangers and pilgrims, abstain from fleshly lusts, which war against the soul"* (1 Pet. 2:9,11).

Prayer: Thank you for the commandments of your Word, O Lord. They are gifts of love to your people to keep us from falling into destruction. Blessed is the individual who fears you, that delights greatly in your commandments.[1] I want to delight in your law at all times.

Lord, sexual immorality is rampant in our land. Remove the darkness from people's hearts.[2] Help them to see that you are able to fill the needs of their hearts so that they will not seek to fill these needs with sexual immorality or any other sin.

Therefore, O Lord, send your Holy Spirit and your anointed messengers to seek and to save those involved in sexual immorality. Prepare the hearts of the sinners to respond and to turn from darkness to light,[3] to receive Jesus Christ as their personal Lord and Savior,[4] to stand fast in the liberty wherewith Christ has set them free and to not be entangled again in the yoke of the bondage of sexual sin.[5]

I lift up to you the following individual(s) who is (are) involved in sexual immorality: _____
_____ . Lead him/her (they/them) back to you, Father. Draw him/her (they/them) unto yourself so that he/she (they/them) will be able to resist the devil in the full knowledge that he will then flee from him/her (they/them).[6] Let no man say when he is tempted, I am tempted by you, O Lord; for I know that you cannot be tempted with evil, and I know that you do not tempt any man or woman or young person.[7]

Help our young people to flee youthful lusts[8] instead of running after them. Restore the values of purity and chastity to this generation. Convict those who are involved in sexual immorality of the truth that fornication is a sin. He who commits fornication sins against his own body.[9] Let the plague of AIDS and other sexually transmitted diseases reveal this truth to our people today.

Lord, I know it grieves you to see so many Christians falling prey to sexual immorality as well. Restore holy vision and a desire for purity to your people, enabling them to understand that their bodies are the temple of your Holy Spirit who lives within them.[10]

Deliver our nation from evil in the form of sexual immorality, Lord.[11] Restore traditional, Christian values to our country. May we once again see family values taking high priority, a return to monogamy and a realization that sex is a gift from you, Father, a gift that is to be enjoyed within the confines of a marriage of mutual honor, love, trust and commitment. Amen.

References: *(1)Psalms 112:1; (2)Colossians 1:13; (3)Acts 26:18; (4)John 1:12; (5)Galatians 5:1; (6)James 4:7-8; (7)James 1:13; (8)2 Timothy 2:22; (9)1 Corinthians 6:18-19; (10)1 Corinthians 6:19-20; (11)Luke 11:4.*

Spiritual Blindness

Key Thought: "I once was blind, but now I see."

Key Scripture: *"This I say therefore, and testify in the Lord, that ye henceforth walk not as other Gentiles walk, in the vanity of their mind, Having the understanding darkened, being alienated from the life of God through the ignorance that is in them, because of the blindness of their heart: Who being past feeling have given themselves over unto lasciviousness, to work all uncleanness with greediness. But ye have not so learned Christ"* (Eph. 4:18-20).

Prayer: Continue to open my eyes, O Lord, that I may be able to perceive more and more of your truth and love. Help me to always walk in the light of your Word for I know your Word is a lamp unto my feet and a light unto my path even during this age of darkness.[1]

Thank you for the prophets who have opened the eyes of so many through the centuries. Isaiah asked, "Lord, who hath believed our report? and to whom hath the arm of the Lord been revealed?" You showed him that they could not believe in you because you had blinded their eyes and hardened their hearts. Therefore, they could not see with their eyes nor understand with their hearts.[2] Father, I pray for the people of this nation, that they would acknowledge you and turn their hearts toward you before their eyes are completely blinded and their hearts are irrevocably hardened.

So, Father, I ask you to send your Spirit[3] to all those in our nation who are spiritually blind and especially to _____ who has rejected the news of your gospel. Bring your glorious gospel to them. If your gospel is hid, it is hid to them who are lost. The god of this world has blinded the minds of those who do not believe in you, Lord. I ask you to rebuke Satan in their behalf. Let your light — the light of your glorious gospel — shine upon them.[4]

Pour forth your Spirit of love upon our nation, Lord. Help all those who walk in hatred to realize that they are in darkness because of their hate.[5] Help them to walk out of the kingdom of darkness by entering into your kingdom of light.[6]

Dear Father, God of my Lord Jesus Christ, you are the Father of glory. In the name of Jesus[7] I ask you to give unto each person in America the spirit of wisdom and revelation in the knowledge of you that the eyes of their understanding would be enlightened and they would no longer be spiritually blind.[8] As your light of revelation dawns on them, I pray they would respond in faith and receive Jesus Christ as their Lord.[9]

Lord, I beseech you to send forth an alarm to the citizens of our nation through your watchmen on the wall.[10] Let our people know that it is high time for them to awake from their spiritual slumber, for their salvation is near.

References: (1)Psalms 119:105; (2)John 12:38-40; (3)Proverbs 1:23; (4)2 Corinthians 4:3-4; (5)1 John 2:11; (6)1 Peter 2:9; (7)John 16:23; (8)Ephesians 1:17-18; (9)Colossians 2:6; (10)Isaiah 62:6.

Spiritual Warfare

Key Thought: Only the Church is equipped for this warfare.

Key Scripture: *"Finally, my brethren, be strong in the Lord, and in the power of his might. Put on the whole armour of God, that ye may be able to stand against the wiles of the devil. For we wrestle not against flesh and blood, but against principalities, against powers, against the rulers of the darkness of this world, against spiritual wickedness in high places"* *(Eph. 6:10-12).*

Prayer: Blessed be your name, O Lord. You teach my hands to war and my fingers to fight. You are my goodness and my fortress, my high tower and my deliverer. You are my shield and in you do I put my trust as I engage in spiritual warfare.[1]

All about us, Lord, people are being blinded by the wickedness and selfishness of the age. Thank you for justifying me so that I would be able to live by your faith.[2] Professing themselves to be wise, many in this present age have become fools who have exchanged your uncorruptible glory for idolatry.[3] Therefore, you have given them up to uncleanness and vile affections.[4] Lord, I beseech you to stem the tide of wickedness in our nation and the world.

Thank you, Father, for revealing to your people the truth about spiritual warfare. Help us to remember that spiritual warfare requires both offensive and defensive positions. I thank you that you have given your Church authority over the power of the evil one.[5] Praise your name.

Bind the strong man in America, O God, and tear down his strongholds in people's minds and attitudes. Even as you have delivered me from the power of darkness and have translated me into the kingdom of your dear Son, I ask you to deliver the people of our nation. In Jesus — and only in Jesus — do we have redemption through His blood, even the forgiveness of sins.[6] May all those who are alienated from you by their wicked works be reconciled through Jesus, our precious Savior.[7]

Father, help your Church to redeem the time because the days are evil.[8] Continue to lead us to wage warfare in the power of your Spirit, through prayer, the Word of your truth and the matchless name of Jesus. Help us to be true intercessors for our nation and the Church. Thank you for your Word which is quick and powerful and sharper than any two-edged sword.[9]

As we go forth into the warfare that is all around us, we do so wielding the weapon of your Word. We are reminded that this is exactly how you defeated the enemy, Lord Jesus, by saying, "It is written...."[10] I am persuaded that neither death, nor life, nor angels, nor principalities, nor powers, nor things present, nor things to come, nor height, nor depth, nor any other creature, shall be able to separate us from your love, Christ Jesus my Lord. In all these things we are more than conquerors through you.[11] Praise your name!

Lord, you are so faithful to me and to all my brothers and sisters. You are establishing me and your people and you are keeping us from evil.[12] Now unto you, the King eternal, immortal, invisible, the only wise God, I give honor and glory for ever and ever.[13]

Thank you for bringing your salvation to the world, Lord Jesus. Thank you for teaching us that, denying ungodliness and worldly lusts, we should live soberly, righteously and godly in this present world, looking for the blessed hope and glorious appearing of the One who is our Savior — you, the Lord Jesus Christ who gave yourself for us that you would redeem us from all iniquity and purify unto yourself a peculiar people, zealous of good works.[14]

Help us, God, to expose the works of darkness whenever we encounter them,[15] to resist the devil in the full knowledge that he will flee from us,[16] to be sober and vigilant because we know our adversary, the devil, as a roaring lion, walks about, seeking whom he may devour.[17]

Your Word declares that we overcome Satan by the blood of the Lamb and by the word of our testimony[18]; and that we have authority through the name of Jesus.[19] Guide us as we resist him, steadfast in the faith, knowing that you, Father, are greater than he is.[20] All power in heaven and in earth has been given unto Jesus, O God, and because He lives within me, I can avail myself of your exceeding power to defeat the enemy.[21] Greater are you who dwells within us than he who is in the world.[22]

I thank you and praise you that you have spoiled principalities and powers, and that you have made a show of them openly.[23] Nothing is too hard for you.[24] Your works are great and honorable and glorious, and your righteousness endures forever.[25] Therefore, I praise you with all my heart in the assembly of the upright and in the congregation,[26] as I realize that no weapon formed against me will prosper.[27]

References: (1)Psalms 144:1-2; (2)Romans 1:17; (3)Romans 1:22-23; (4)Romans 1:24,26; (5)Matthew 28:18-20; (6)Colossians 1:13-14; (7)Colossians 1:21; (8)Ephesians 5:16; (9)Hebrews 4:12; (10)Matthew 4; (11)Romans 8:37-39; (12)2 Thessalonians 3:3; (13)1 Timothy 1:17; (14)Titus 2:11-14; (15)Ephesians 5:11; (16)James 4:7; (17)1 Peter 5:8; (18)Revelation 12:11; (19)Mark 16:17 and Luke 10:17; (20)1 Peter 5:9; (21)Matthew 28:18; (22)1 John 4:4; (23)Colossians 2:15; (24)Genesis 18:14; (25)Psalms 112:3; (26)Psalms 111:1; (27)Isaiah 54:17.

Stresses

Key Thought: God's gracious invitation is for us to cast all our cares upon Him.

Key Scripture: *"Casting all your care upon him; for he careth for you"* *(1 Pet. 5:7).*

Prayer: Thank you, Lord Jesus, that your yoke is easy and your burden is light. As I take your yoke upon me and learn of you, I am freed from the burdens and stresses and cares of this life. I ask you to open the ears of my fellow Americans so that they will hear your invitation to come unto you, the great Burden-Bearer, and leave their troubles with you.[1]

How I thank you, heavenly Father, that you answered me in the day of my distress. You were with me then and you have been with me ever since.[2] Be with my fellow citizens during this stressful time. Lead the unemployed, homeless, distressed, and the otherwise burdened people of my country to cry out to you in their distress.[3] Help them,[4] comfort them[5] and be their supply[6] in time of trouble.

Even as the faith of the Thessalonians brought comfort to Paul and Timothy during their time of affliction and distress, I ask you to comfort all your people in America today. I believe you are hearing and answering my prayer even now.[7]

From personal experience and from your Word, I know that neither death, nor life, nor angels, nor principalities, nor powers, nor things present, nor things to come, nor height, nor depth, nor any other creature, shall be able to separate me from your love, Lord Jesus Christ.[8] There is no stress too great to be perfectly handled by you, my Savior. Thank you for your overwhelming love.

God, you are so good to us and you have been good to the United States of America. I pray that your goodness would continue in our country, that you would lead us all to the place of recognizing your majestic sovereignty.[9]

Help the citizens of our nation to become disciples of our Lord and Savior Jesus Christ. Then guide them by your Word not to be anxious or to worry, but in all situations by prayer and supplication, with thanksgiving, to let their requests be made known unto you, O God, so that your peace will keep their hearts and minds through Christ Jesus.[10]

When David cried out in his distress and called upon your holy name, you heard his voice and his cry entered your ears. It was then that the earth shook and trembled. The foundations of heaven moved and shook because of your anger.[11] Help your people in this land to follow his example, fully believing that you are our Rock. In you shall we trust because you are our shield and the horn of our salvation. You are our high tower and our refuge. You are our Savior and you have promised to save us from all violence.[12] I praise your most holy name.

References: *(1)Matthew 11:28; (2)Genesis 35:3; (3)Psalms 18:6; (4)Psalms 46:1; (5)2 Corinthians 1:3; (6)Philippians 4:19; (7)1 Thessalonians 3:7; (8)Romans 8:38-39; (9)Hebrews 8:1; (10)Philippians 4:6-7; (11)2 Samuel 22:7-8; (12)2 Samuel 22:3.*

Teachers

Key Thought: Education without God is like a ship without a compass.

Key Scripture: *"Bow down thine ear, and hear the words of the wise, and apply thine heart unto my knowledge. For it is a pleasant thing if thou keep them within thee"* (Prov. 22:17-18).

Prayer: Thank you for the teachers of our land, those men and women who labor diligently to train our children, young people and adults in various disciplines of study. Help them to follow your counsel and to seek your knowledge that they might know the certainty of your words of truth.[1] You have established a testimony in Jacob and appointed a law in Israel — a law which you have commanded to our fathers, that they should make them known unto their children.[2] Help our teachers to realize that this is their responsibility as well — to show to the generations the praises of your name, to reveal your strength and your wonderful works that you have done.[3]

The entrance of your words gives light, O Lord. It gives understanding to all.[4] May your Word of truth find its rightful place in our schools today and may our teachers remember that your Word is a lamp unto their feet and a light unto their pathway.[5] Let your commandments make them wise, Father, and become the rejoicing of our teacher's hearts.[6]

Because they care, many teachers inspire and motivate their students to seek the truth and to reach for understanding. Help them to realize the importance of their calling, to see that they are role models for their students and to take that responsibility very seriously before you. Show our teachers that they can do all things through the Lord Jesus Christ.[7] You will keep them in perfect peace whose minds are stayed on you because they trust in you.[8]

Be a very present help[9] to all our teachers, Lord — those in pre-school programs, kindergarten, elementary schools, middle schools, junior and senior high schools, home schools, colleges and universities, seminaries, graduate and post-graduate schools and Sunday schools. Inspire them and guide them. Bless them in their important work. Help them to keep from growing weary in well-doing.[10] Inspire and anoint the teachers of your Word by filling them with your Spirit, Lord.[11]

Blessed are all those who trust in you, Lord. May each teacher in our land learn to trust you and find his or her hope in you.[12] Let them keep your commandments, for length of days, long life and peace will they add to their lives.[13] Help our teachers to excel at establishing caring relationships with their pupils.[14] As they gather the children,[15] help teachers to share your statutes, O God, and to observe your laws.[16] May they never forget the principles and values that have made our nation great — honesty, faith, love, hard work and discipline. In so doing, Lord, may they stamp your name upon their students so that you can bless them.[17]

Father, I ask that your Word would increase and the number of your disciples would multiply greatly among the teachers in America and as a result, an overwhelming majority would become obedient to the faith[18] loving you with all their hearts.[19]

References: (1)Proverbs 22:20; (2)Psalms 78:5; (3)Psalms 78:4; (4)Psalms 119:130; (5)Psalms 119:105; (6)Psalms 119:98; (7)Philippians 4:13; (8)Isaiah 26:3; (9)Psalms 46:1; (10)2 Thessalonians 3:13; (11)Ephesians 5:18; (12)Jeremiah 17:7; (13)Proverbs 3:1-2; (14)1 Peter 3:8; (15)Joel 2:16; (16)Exodus 18:16; (17)Deuteronomy 28:10-11; (18)Acts 6:7; (19)Mark 12:30.

Terrorism

Key Thought: The god of terrorists is destruction.

Key Scripture: *"The God of my rock; in him will I trust: he is my shield, and the horn of my salvation, my high tower, and my refuge, my saviour; thou savest me from violence. I will call on the Lord, who is worthy to be praised: so shall I be saved from mine enemies."* *(2 Sam. 22:3-4).*

Prayer: Heavenly Father, we are living in an age when terrorism is disrupting the lives of many around the world. I come against the evil spirit of terrorism in the name of Jesus. Father, I ask you to overthrow the violent terrorists according to your Word.[1]

The land is full of bloody crimes, Lord, and the cities are full of violence.[2] I thank you for your promise that all those who live by the sword shall perish with the sword.[3] Lead those who take captives into captivity themselves.[4] Let pangs and sorrows overtake them, and let the terrorists be in pain as a woman in labor.[5]

Heavenly Father, I ask you to intervene in miraculous ways whenever terrorists plan to riot, take hostages, hijack vehicles, bomb airplanes, vehicles or buildings or participate in other evil actions. Thwart their plans, Lord, and protect the innocent.[6]

You are our eternal refuge, heavenly Father, and you have promised to thrust out the enemy before us.[7] Gracious God, I love you and I praise you for your protection. You will bless the righteous and your favor will compass us as with a shield.[8] Your people do not have to be afraid of sudden fear, neither of the desolation of the wicked, when it comes. Because you are our confidence and you will keep our feet from being taken.[9] I praise you for the promises of your Word, Father.

Open the eyes of Americans today, Lord, so that they will understand that you are nigh unto all who call upon you in truth. You preserve all who love you, but you will destroy the wicked.[10] Show the people of our land that all who hearken unto you shall dwell safely and be quiet from all fear of evil.[11] You will preserve our going out and our coming in from this time forth and forevermore.[12] Hallelujah! What a Savior!

Thank you for sending your angels to protect us. They encamp around all who fear you, Father, and they deliver us from evil.[13] When the enemy of our souls uses terrorism to distract your people by filling them with fear, I ask you to lift up a standard against him.[14] You are our shield, and you are our exceeding great reward.[15] Thank you for your promise to deliver your people out of the hand of all enemies.[16]

Minister your comfort[17] to all those who have been victimized by terrorism in our land and be with their families.[18] Watch over the families of those who were killed as a result of terroristic activities. Impart your wisdom to our leaders so that they would know how to deal with terrorism in the most effective manner possible.[19]

Help America to acknowledge once again that our help is in your name, O Lord.[20] Your right hand shall save us.[21] Your name is a strong tower, and when the righteous run into it, they shall be kept safe.[22] You are an everlasting shield to all who put their trust in you.[23]

References: (1)Psalms 140:11; (2)Ezekiel 7:23; (3)Matthew 26:52; (4)Revelation 13:10; (5)Isaiah 13:8; (6)Deuteronomy 19:10; (7)Deuteronomy 33:27; (8)Psalms 5:12; (9)Proverbs 3:25-26; (10)Psalms 145:18-20; (11)Proverbs 1:33; (12)Psalms 121:8; (13)Psalms 34:7; (14)Isaiah 59:19; (15)Genesis 15:1; (16)2 Kings 17:39; (17)2 Corinthians 1:3; (18)Psalms 46:1; (19)Proverbs 2:6; (20)Psalms 124:8; (21)Psalms 138:7; (22)Proverbs 18:10; (23)Proverbs 30:5.

Those Who Mourn

Key Thought: Death teaches us the importance of love.

Key Scripture: *"To appoint unto them that mourn in Zion, to give unto them beauty for ashes, the oil of joy for mourning, the garment of praise for the spirit of heaviness; that they might be called trees of righteousness, the planting of the Lord, that he might be glorified"* *(Isa. 61:3).*

Prayer: Heavenly Father, I pray for all who mourn the losses of loved ones in our land today. I thank you for your promise that the time will come when we will no longer need to mourn, a time when we will not need to weep, when our tears will not need to flow.[1] Bless those who mourn, Lord Jesus, and let them know that their comfort will come.[2] I pray especially for _____
who knows the pain of mourning at this present time. Comfort him/her with your love. Help him/her to see that you will turn the wilderness into Eden, the desert into the garden of your grace.[3]

Help those of us who know you, Lord Jesus, to comfort one another with the joyous knowledge that you will return. Thank you, Jesus. You will descend with a shout, with the voice of the archangel, and with the trump of God, and the dead in you will rise first, then we which are alive and remain shall be caught up together with them in the clouds to meet you and so shall we ever be with you.[4]

You, Lord, are the one who comforts us. You divided the sea and you love your people.[5] Thank you for giving your children the Holy Spirit to be our Comforter. You have promised that He will abide with us forever. Spirit of Truth, abide with us forever. Though the world cannot receive you because it cannot see you and cannot know you, I know that you dwell with your people and you shall always be with us. Thank you for not leaving your people comfortless as we await your return, Lord Jesus.[6]

Blessed be your name, Father, for you are the Father of all mercies, the God of all comfort.[7] You comfort us in all our tribulation so that we may be able to comfort them who are in trouble in any form by the comfort wherewith you have comforted us.[8] I pray for all those who are in any kind of trouble or loss, that you would bless them with comfort. Help me, Lord, to comfort others with the same comfort you have given to me through the blessed hope of your appearing.[9]

Father, comfort all those who are cast down.[10] Because you have filled me with comfort I am able to be exceeding joyful even in tribulation. Therefore, great is my boldness of speech and prayer.[11] Help my fellow Americans to know this same joy. Comfort others with the same comfort you have given to me through the blessed hope of your appearing.[9]

Lord, I cry unto you in behalf of all those who mourn. Give ear unto my voice. Let my prayer be set forth before you as incense, and the lifting up of my hands as the evening sacrifice.[12] Let all those who seek you rejoice and be glad in you. May you be magnified in our land and throughout the earth.[13]

References: (1)Ezekiel 24:16; (2)Matthew 5:4; (3)Isaiah 51:3; (4)1 Thessalonians 4:17-18; (5)Psalms 136:13; (6)John 14:16-18; (7)2 Corinthians 1:3; (8)2 Corinthians 1:4; (9)Titus 2:13; (10)2 Corinthians 7:6; (11)2 Corinthians 7:4; (12)Psalms 141:1-2; (13)Psalms 70:4.

Truth, Honesty and Integrity

Key Thought: The truth is always the strongest argument.

Key Scripture: *"My son, forget not my law; but let thine heart keep my commandments: For length of days, and long life, and peace, shall they add to thee. Let not mercy and truth forsake thee: bind them about thy neck; write them upon the table of thine heart: So shalt thou find favour and good understanding in the sight of God and man"* *(Prov. 3:1-4).*

Prayer: Lord, bring back the values of truth, honesty and integrity to the people of our land. You are the way, the truth, the life; and no one can come to the Father except through you.[1] You said that we would know the truth and the truth would make us free.[2]

Lead me and all the citizens of our nation to the truth; may we ever honor and uphold the truth in all our dealings with our fellow men. Speaking your truth in love, Lord Jesus, help us to grow up into you in all things.[3] Convict all those who bear false witnesses against their neighbors of their sin and convince them of the need to tell the truth.[4] Make it clear to the liars in our land that a false witness will not go unpunished and he that speaks lies shall not escape.[5]

Let integrity and uprightness preserve our nation, Lord. Redeem the United States of America, O God, out of all our troubles[6] and forgive us of our iniquities.[7]

Judge us, O Lord, according to our integrity. Lead the people of our nation to trust in you so that we will never slide from the special position you have prepared for us.[8] As for me, with your help, I will walk in my integrity. Redeem me and be merciful unto me and the country that I love.[9]

Reveal your truth to the people of our nation, Lord. Show them that a false balance is an abomination to you, but a just weight is your delight. Teach our citizens and leaders that selfish pride brings shame, but with the lowly there is wisdom. Let the integrity of the upright guide them.[10] Remind our people that the just walk in integrity and their children are blessed after them.[11]

As we learn to pray for our leaders faithfully, Lord, you promise that we will be able to lead a quiet and peaceable life in all godliness and honesty.[12] Help us to be faithful in this commission, Father, and I ask you to raise up many intercessors in our land. Give us the peace, honesty and godliness that you have promised to a people who put you first.

Lord, the night is far spent and the day is at hand. Help our nation to cast off the works of darkness and to put on the armor of light. Let us walk honestly, as in the day.[13] Teach us to study to be quiet, to mind our own business and to work with our own hands as you have commanded us to do. By so doing, Lord, we will be able to walk honestly toward them that are without and we will lack no good thing.[14]

As we allow you to live in our hearts, your truth, honesty and integrity will flow forth in our lives. Unto you, O God, do I lift up my soul. O my God, I trust in you; let me not be ashamed, let not my enemies triumph over me. I praise you for the truth that none who wait on you shall be ashamed. Let those who deliberately transgress your law be ashamed. Show me your ways, O Lord; teach me your paths. Lead me in your truth and teach me, for you are the God of my salvation; on you do I wait all the day.[15] Be exalted, O God, above the heavens and let your glory shine over all the earth.[16]

References: *(1)John 14:6; (2)John 8:32; (3)Ephesians 4:15; (4)Exodus 20:16; (5)Proverbs 19:5; (6)Psalms 25:21-22; (7)Psalms 103:3; (8)Psalms 26:1; (9)Psalms 26:11; (10)Proverbs 11:1-3; (11)Proverbs 20:7; (12)1 Timothy 2:2; (13)Romans 13:12-13; (14)1 Thessalonians 4:11-12; (15)Psalms 25:1-5; (16)Psalms 108:1-5.*

The United States of America

Key Thought: One nation under God.

Key Scripture: *"Ye are the light of the world. A city that is set on an hill cannot be hid. . . . Let your light so shine before men, that they may see your good works, and glorify your Father which is in heaven"* (Matt. 5:14,16).

Prayer: Thank you, Father, for the United States of America — a city that has been set on a hill by your hand of purpose. God, bless America, the land that I love. Stand beside her and guide her with a light from above. Guard my country, Lord, so that the forces of wickedness and immorality will be destroyed within its boundaries, and the standard of holiness will be raised for all to see.

Strengthen the bars of our gates, O Lord. Bless our children. May our harvest be plentiful and our granaries be full so that we will be able to share with all in need. Send forth your commandments to our land so that people will hear your Word and be glad. You have not dealt so graciously and bountifully with any other nation as you have dealt with our country, O Lord, and I thank you and praise you.[1] May the purple mountains' majesty and the amber waves of grain continue to show forth your glory.

Stay your hand of judgment, Lord. Lead your people to pray for their nation, and help all people to realize that our country was established to be one nation under you. If your people — the ones who are called by your name

— will humble themselves and pray and seek your face, and turn from their wicked ways, then you will hear from heaven and you will forgive our sins and heal our land.[2] Thank you for calling me, Father. I repent before you this day as I endeavor to seek your face through prayer. Please heal our land.

You are known in part by the judgments you execute. The wicked are often snared in the works of their own hands. You have declared that the wicked shall be turned into hell, and that any nation that forgets you will receive your judgment. Arise, O Lord; let not man prevail. Put them in fear, O God. Deliver us from arrogance and help our country's leaders to know that they are your servants.[3]

Lord, you are high above all nations. Your glory is above the heavens.[4] Father, you have declared that Jesus Christ is your only begotten Son,[5] that He has supernatural power according to the spirit of holiness by the resurrection of the dead. Through Him we have received grace to be obedient to the faith among all nations.[6] I pray that your Son will pour forth His grace upon the United States of America so that the spirit of holiness will fill our land and our people will become obedient to the faith that was once delivered to the saints.[7]

As your Word points out, many people of the land have used oppression, and exercised robbery, and have vexed the poor and needy. Many have also oppressed the stranger wrongfully. But, Lord, you seek for someone among us who should make up the hedge and stand in the gap before you for the land so that you would not destroy it. I pray, loving and merciful Father, that you will call forth many intercessors for America who will stand in the gap before you. May I always be one of that growing number of intercessors.[8]

Thank you for hearing the cry of the righteous who pray night and day for our nation. In the same way that you responded to the cries of Abraham when he asked you to spare the city because of the righteous who lived there, please spare America because of those faithful servants who are taking a stand for righteousness in a time when it is not popular to do so.[9]

Mighty Lord, call forth many prophets in this hour who will courageously speak forth your Word and your warnings to our people. Instill them with holy boldness to proclaim the truth, even in the face of opposition. Give me courage to take a stand against unrighteousness in all its hideous forms. May I be like Asa who responded to the Word of God with courage by putting away all the abominable idols out of the land of Judah and Benjamin.[10]

Inspire us and empower us with your Spirit, Lord, to be of good courage and to fear not. Help me to keep and to do all that is written in your law. I desire with all my heart to stay on track, never turning aside from your will, either to the right or to the left. I cleave to you, O Lord, for you are able to drive out before us great and strong nations. No man shall stand before you, but with your Spirit one man is able to chase a thousand because you are fighting for us.[11]

I will bless you at all times. Your praise shall be continually in my mouth.[12] Blessed is the nation whose God is you, O Lord.[13] May the United States of America ever be that nation, a country in which no other gods are put before you,[14] a land that honors you and serves you. May our leaders remember that no king is saved by the multitude of a host,[15] and that your eye is upon those who fear you, upon those who hope in your mercy.[16] Have mercy upon us, O Lord.[17]

Thank you that you hear when the righteous cry,[18] and you deliver the righteous out of all their troubles. Lord, my heart breaks for the sin and blindness of my nation. But I thank you that you are near to all who are of a broken heart and save all those of a contrite spirit.[19] I love you, O Lord my God.

References: *(1)Psalms 147:13-20; (2)2 Chronicles 7:14; (3)Psalms 9:17-20; (4)Psalms 113:4; (5)John 3:16; (6)Romans 1:4-5; (7)Jude 3; (8)Ezekiel 22:29-31; (9)Genesis 18:27-33; (10)2 Chronicles 15:7-8; (11)Joshua 23:8-12; (12)Psalms 34:1; (13)Psalms 33:12; (14)Deuteronomy 5:7; (15)Psalms 33:16; (16)Psalms 33:16-18; (17)Psalms 51:1; (18)Psalms 34:15; (19)Psalms 34:18.*

Victims

Key Thought: "No one can make you feel inferior without your permission" (Eleanor Roosevelt).

Key Scripture: *"The Lord also will be a refuge for the oppressed, a refuge in times of trouble. And they that know thy name will put their trust in thee: for thou, Lord, hast not forsaken them that seek thee"* (Ps. 9:9-10).

Prayer: Heavenly Father, Father of our Lord Jesus Christ, I come to you now in behalf of all those who perceive themselves to be victims and all those who actually are victims in our society today — victims of injustice, abuse, crime, disease, mental conditions, malpractice, fraud, misunderstanding, etc. Be a very present help to them, O Lord.[1] I thank you that you never forsake those who seek you.[2]

Judge the poor of the people. Save the children of the needy. Break in pieces the oppressors.[3] Look upon us and be merciful to us. Deliver each victim, Father, from the oppression of man and Satan, and help us all to keep your precepts.[4] Bring healing to the broken-hearted and set the captives free.[5]

I know, O Lord, that your judgments are right. Let your tender mercies flow to those who are oppressed and let the proud be ashamed, for they have dealt perversely with victims without a cause.[6] Empower us to fight against the oppressors in our land, O Lord, for your Word declares that if we will fight, we shall be remembered by you and we shall be saved from our enemies.[7]

He who oppresses the victims in our land reproaches you, O Lord. Drive the wicked away in their wickedness. Help us all to remember that righteousness exalts a nation, but sin is a reproach to any people.[8] Exalt the United States through the righteousness of its leaders and people, and drive out all the wicked oppressors from our land.

Father, spread the seeds of your Word throughout our nation. Your Word will not return to you void; you will accomplish your purposes as we learn to follow you.[9] Wash the people of our land in your Word.[10] Make them clean. Put away the evildoers from before your eyes. Teach all of us how to cease from doing evil and to learn to do well. Show us how to relieve the victims of their suffering.[11]

I pray particularly for _____ _____ who is/are a victim(s) of _____ . Be close to him/her/them as they endeavor to find answers for their problems. Bring concerned Christians into their lives so that they can be ministered to in your love, Lord. As victims hear your Word proclaimed, may they respond in faith to your message of salvation. Save them[12] and heal them of their wounds[13] as they learn to place their trust in Jesus Christ.[14] Amen.

References: *(1)Psalms 46:1; (2)Psalms 9:10; (3)Psalms 72:4; (4)Psalms 119:134; (5)Isaiah 61:1; (6)Psalms 119:76-79; (7)Numbers 10:9; (8)Proverbs 14:34; (9)Isaiah 55:11; (10)Ephesians 5:26; (11)Isaiah 1:16-17; (12)John 3:16; (13)Luke 4:18; (14)Ephesians 1:13.*

Violence in Our Land

Key Thought: Man's wrath never works righteousness.

Key Scripture: *"Violence shall no more be heard in thy land, wasting nor destruction within thy borders; but thou shalt call thy walls Salvation, and thy gates Praise....the Lord shall be unto thee an everlasting light, and thy God thy glory"* *(Isa. 60:18-19).*

Prayer: Lord God, you are our refuge and strength, a very present help in trouble. Therefore, I will not fear, though the earth be removed, and though the mountains be carried into the midst of the sea.[1] You are my rock, my fortress and my deliverer. In you do I trust. You are my shield, and the horn of my salvation, my high tower, and my refuge. You are my Savior and you save me from all violence.[2] Thank you, Father, for all you are to me.

When I call on you, Lord, so shall I be saved from my enemies.[3] You are my lamp, O Lord, and you will lighten my darkness. Through you I am able to run through a troop and leap over a wall.[4] You are my strength and power, and you make my way perfect.[5] Because I am secure in you, I fear no evil from the violence and wickedness of this present time.

I have seen violence and strife in the cities of our land.[6] Many are afraid to walk the streets at night and even during the day because of drive-by shootings, rapes, rioting, drunkenness, murders, auto thefts, gang violence and many other forms of wickedness. Lord, I ask you to hasten the day when violence will no more be heard in our land, when people will no longer fear the night because you are our everlasting light and our glory.[7] Evening, and morning, and at noon, will I pray, and cry aloud, and I know you will hear my voice.[8]

Thank you, Father, for the promises of your Word. You have declared that you will spare the poor and the needy, and that you shall redeem their souls from deceit and violence.[9] Blessed be your glorious name forever. May America and the whole earth be filled with your glory, O Lord my God.[10]

Those who practice violence and murder will flee to the pit, but those who walk uprightly shall be saved.[11] When violence was done to the Israelites, you, Lord, declared that you would plead their cause and take vengeance for them.[12] I pray, Father, for all the victims of violence in our land, that you would bless them with peace, protection and forgiveness, and that you would take revenge in their behalf.

Vengeance is yours and I ask you to avenge those who are wronged by violence. Give them grace to forgive their oppressors. Thank you for your promise, Lord, that you will repay.[13] Help all those who turn to violence and practice violence to remember that it is a fearful thing to fall into your hands, O living God.[14]

O Lord God, to whom vengeance belongs, show yourself to the people of our land. Lift up yourself, Judge of the earth, and render a reward to the proud.[15] I know that you will not allow the wicked to triumph. You will bring upon them their own iniquity, and shall cut them off in their own wickedness.[16] Thank you, Lord.

Fill our nation with your loving presence, for your lovingkindness is better than life.[17] Because you have been my help, therefore in the shadow of your wings I will rejoice. My soul follows hard after you, and your right hand holds me up. But those who seek my soul, to destroy it, shall go to the lower parts of the earth. They shall fall by the sword, and they shall be a portion for foxes. The leaders of our nation will rejoice in you. Everyone who commits their way to you shall glory in you, but the mouth of them who speak lies and do violence shall be stopped.[18] Thank you, Jesus.

References: (1)Psalms 46:1-2; (2)2 Samuel 22:2-3; (3)2 Samuel 22:4; (4)2 Samuel 22:30; (5)2 Samuel 22:32-33; (6)Psalms 55:9; (7)Isaiah 60:19; (8)Psalms 55:17; (9)Psalms 72:13-14; (10)Psalms 72:18-19; (11)Proverbs 28:17-18; (12)Jeremiah 51:35-36; (13)Hebrews 10:30; (14)Hebrews 10:31; (15)Psalms 94:1-2; (16)Psalms 94:23; (17)Psalms 63:3; (18)Psalms 63:7-11.

Wisdom

Key Thought: Wisdom is knowing what to do next; skill is knowing how to do it; virtue is doing it.

Key Scripture: *"Wisdom is the principal thing; therefore get wisdom: and with all thy getting get understanding....she shall bring thee to honour, when thou dost embrace her" (Prov. 4:7-8).*

Prayer: Loving God, help our nation — both its leaders and its citizens — to realize that the fear of you is the beginning of wisdom,[1] and that wisdom is a tree of life to all who obtain it.[2] You put wisdom in the hearts of your people, Lord, and I ask you to fill the hearts of Americans with your wisdom.[3]

Help all of us to see the important connection you have made between spiritual understanding and wisdom. Give our leaders understanding hearts to judge the people of our nation. Enable our people to discern between good and bad, right and wrong.[4] Thank you for the example you've given us in your Word of King Solomon, the wisest man on the face of the earth. He knew how to make right judgments because your wisdom was within him.[5] King Solomon surpassed all the kings of the earth in both riches and wisdom.[6]

The price of wisdom is above rubies, Lord.[7] It cannot be gotten for gold, neither shall silver be weighed for its price.[8] Teach us to number our days, that we may apply our hearts unto wisdom.[9] Help me and all believers to learn to hold our peace so that you can teach us your precious wisdom.

I thank you for your Word, Father. It is a treasure trove of wisdom and other riches. Out of your mouth come both knowledge and understanding.[10] Restore respect for your Word to the people of our land.

I thank you that the happiest people are those who have found wisdom and received understanding from you.[11] All the things a person can desire cannot be compared unto wisdom.[12] I thank you, Father, that length of days is in wisdom's right hand and riches and honor are in wisdom's left hand.[13] You have taught us that the ways of wisdom are ways of pleasantness and its pathways are paved by peace.[14] Wisdom is a tree of life to all who lay hold upon it.[15] Bring wisdom to our land, Lord. Fill our leaders, teachers, young people and others with your wisdom.

Help us to value wisdom in America once more, Lord. May our nation never forsake wisdom because wisdom will preserve us. If our people will learn to love wisdom, you will keep us strong.[16] Wisdom will bring honor to our land. Help our people to embrace wisdom once again.[17]

Through wisdom kings are able to reign and princes are able to decree justice. Impart wisdom to our leaders, Almighty God, so that they will be able to rule more effectively and to judge righteously.[18]

All who find your wisdom, Lord, find the abundant life that you have promised to your people and they obtain favor from you.[19]

Those who sin against your wisdom by acting foolishly or selfishly wrong their own souls[20] and it would seem that they love death more than life.[21] Help the people of our nation to understand that there are many ways that seem right to people, but the ends thereof are the ways of death.[22]

Help our leaders and people to see the relationship between justice and wisdom for it is the mouth of the just that brings forth your wisdom, Lord.[23] How I thank you, Lord Jesus, that your wisdom is greater than that of Solomon,[24] and that you have promised to impart wisdom to all those who ask you for it.[25] I ask you for your wisdom to be poured forth upon our land by your Holy Spirit. Send your wisdom to help our leaders and citizens solve the problems our nation faces. In so doing, Father, may all our people receive Christ Jesus, who has been made unto us wisdom.[26] Amen.

References: (1)*Psalms 111:10;* (2)*Proverbs 3:18;* (3)*Exodus 31:6;* (4)*1 Kings 3:9;* (5)*1 Kings 3:28;* (6)*2 Chronicles 9:22;* (7)*Job 28:18;* (8)*Job 28:15;* (9)*Psalms 90:12;* (10)*Proverbs 2:6;* (11)*Proverbs 3:13;* (12)*Proverbs 3:15;* (13)*Proverbs 3:16;* (14)*Proverbs 3:17;* (15)*Proverbs 3:18;* (16)*Proverbs 4:6;* (17)*Proverbs 4:8;* (18)*Proverbs 8:15-16;* (19)*Proverbs 8:35;* (20)*Proverbs 8:36;* (21)*Proverbs 8:36;* (22)*Proverbs 14:12;* (23)*Proverbs 10:31;* (24)*Matthew 12:42;* (25)*James 1:5;* (26)*1 Corinthians 1:30.*

Young People

Key Thought: It's better to build a child than to mend an adult.

Key Scripture: *"Let no man despise thy youth: but be thou an example of the believers, in word, in conversation, in charity, in spirit, in faith, in purity. Till I come, give attendance to reading, to exhortation, to doctrine. Neglect not the gift that is in thee, which was given thee by prophecy, with the laying on of the hands of the presbytery. Meditate upon these things: give thyself wholly to them; that thy profiting may appear to all"* (1 Tim. 4:12-15).

Prayer: Wonderful Lord, I thank you for the young people of our nation. Help me to be an encouragement to them at all times, to look for their potential instead of their faults, to be an example unto them and a prayer warrior in their behalf.

I thank you for the many examples in the Scriptures of young people who did mighty exploits in your name, for David, Joshua, Joseph, Stephen, Timothy and many others who surrendered their lives totally to you. Challenge our young people today, Lord Jesus, to take up their cross and follow you.[1] Help them to flee youthful lusts,[2] and to remember you — their Creator — in the days of their youth.[3]

I thank you, Lord, for the many young people across America who are setting a godly standard before their peers and doing exploits for their God.[4] Strengthen them by your Spirit in their inner man.[5] Protect, encourage, bless and enable them that they may not grow weary in well doing, but may reap the fruit of faithfulness.[6]

Turn the hearts of our young people toward you, Father, so that they might ask with David of old, "How shall a young person cleanse his or her way?" Your answer remains the same now as it was then, Lord, "...by taking heed thereto according to your Word."[7] In our present day there are so many forces of ungodliness that seek to seduce our youth in the form of peer-group pressure, rebellion, distrust, drugs, immorality and so forth. Convict our young people of their need for your righteousness, Lord, so that they will be able to stand in the evil day.[8]

I pray especially for the following young people whom I care about and I know you love: _____ _____ . Be a very present help to them, Lord Jesus, and help them to know your reality and your tender, loving care.[9]

Let the young people of our land rejoice in their youth, and may their hearts cheer them as they walk in the ways of your heart, O Lord. Help them to remember that you behold them at all times and that you love them.[10]

Lord, I make intercession in behalf of our young people, asking you to remind them that you are the guide of their youth.[11] Thank you for your promise that you will remember your covenant with your people in the days of their youth, and that you will establish with them an everlasting covenant.[12]

Reach our young people now, heavenly Father, with the truth of your gospel. Bless youth workers with a special anointing to lead many young people into your kingdom.

I pray for a revival among the young people of America today, a revival that will lead them to receive Jesus Christ as their Lord[13] and to honor their parents while they are still young.[14] May millions of young people in our country be able to say that they have kept your commandments from their youth onward.[15] May the vast majority of our young people become committed Christians.

Heavenly Father, turn the hearts of the parents to their young people and the hearts of the young people to their parents.[16] Show them that rebellion is as the sin of witchcraft in your sight.[17] Help them know that honoring and obeying their parents carries with it the promise that things will be well with them and they will live long on the earth.[18]

Deal bountifully with our young people, Lord, that they may live and keep your Word. Open their eyes that they may behold wondrous things out of your law.[19] Hear my prayer, O Lord. Give ear to my supplications. In your faithfulness answer me, and in your righteousness.[20]

*References: (1) Matthew 16:24; (2)2 Timothy 2:22;
(3)Ecclesiastes 12:1; (4)Daniel 11:32; (5)Ephesians 3:16;
(6)Galatians 6:9; (7)Psalms 119:9-11; (8)John 16:8-10;
(9)Psalms 46:1; (10)Ecclesiastes 11:9-10; (11)Jeremiah 3:4;
(12)Ezekiel 16:60-61; (13)John 1:12; (14)Exodus 20:12;
(15)Matthew 19:19-20; (16)Malachi 4:6; (17)1 Samuel 15:23;
(18)Ephesians 6:1-3; (19)Psalms 119:17-18; (20)Psalms 143:1.*

PRAYERS THAT PREVAIL
FOR AMERICA

Prayer Journal

Date	Notes and Comments

Date	Notes and Comments

Date	Notes and Comments

Date	Notes and Comments

Date	Notes and Comments

Date	Notes and Comments

Date	Notes and Comments

Date	Notes and Comments

Date	Notes and Comments

Date	Notes and Comments

Date	Notes and Comments

Date	Notes and Comments

Date	Notes and Comments

Date	Notes and Comments

Date	Notes and Comments

Date	Notes and Comments

Date	Notes and Comments

Date	Notes and Comments

Date	Notes and Comments

Date	Notes and Comments

Date	Notes and Comments

Date	Notes and Comments

PRAYER CLASSIC

Pray God's Word - Receive His Promises

Praying God's Word puts His dynamic power to work and energizes your faith. PRAYERS THAT PREVAIL is a practical manual for building an effective prayer life. This essential tool is filled with prayers and scriptures that address more than 100 topics of vital concern to every believer.